Moved by Politics

Moved by Politics

12 Episodes in an Academic Life

A Memoir Gerhard Loewenberg

GRAY PEARL PRESS Iowa City, Iowa

Copyright © 2012 Gerhard Loewenberg

Designed by Richard Hendel

Set in Arno Pro, Aller, and Clio types by
Tseng Information Systems, Inc.

ISBN 978-0-9745881-1-7

Contents

Preface / vii

1
Coming to America, 1936 / 1

2
By Subway to the World of Tomorrow / 13

3
The World Beyond New York: Going to College / 21

4
Encountering the Political Science Profession / 33

5
Lessons in the Liberal Arts at Mount Holyoke College / 39

6
Postwar Germany: Questions and Impressions / 53

7
Punch Cards to Computers: The New Language of Political Research / 65

8
The Unsettling Years, 1968–69 / 73

9
Discovering Iowa / 86

10
Founding the *Legislative Studies Quarterly* / 100

11
Unexpectedly Dean / 110

12
Not Quite Retired / 128

Preface

Politics has always moved me, both literally and intellectually. My consistent and continuous interest in politics came out of my early recognition that political events explain why my family and I had to leave the country in which we had lived for generations. A concern for politics therefore originated early in my life and subsequently defined my academic interests. The twelve episodes that I describe in this memoir recall important experiences that shaped the course of my professional life. They reflect the context of growing up in an immigrant family and having a career in the world of higher education as it existed in the second half of the twentieth century. I did not anticipate any of them. They were the important contingent events that explain how my career developed in the context of the time in which I have lived. Each presented unexpected challenges. When I think back on them each provided me with fortunate opportunities and interesting new directions.

This memoir omits most of my personal life, which constitutes the happy background of my professional career. My wife Ina, my children Deborah and Michael, and my close colleagues and friends make only brief appearances in these episodes but that is not meant in any way to overlook the decisive influence they have had on me and my huge indebtedness to them. That would be another story.

I had first written an account of how I obtained my first faculty position, at Mount Holyoke College in 1953, thinking today's graduate students looking for their first jobs might find that interesting. Ina suggested that I might write about other beginnings in my academic life and that together they would describe the turnings that my career took. That turned out to be the inspiration for this book. Kate Gleeson, an accomplished editor, nudged me to go beyond a factual

PREFACE

description of events in each case to describe some of what was in my mind when opportunities and challenges arose. She taught me a thing or two that I needed to learn about the difference between the writing I have done in political science and telling stories about my life. Holly Carver gave me excellent advice on publishing this memoir, and Joan Stearns expertly polished the manuscript. I am indebted to each of them for what has been an enjoyable project.

1

Coming to America, 1936

The sequence of events that caused me to come to America began in September 1935 when my parents and I returned home to Germany from a vacation in Italy. They had surprised me just short of my seventh birthday by taking me along on their trip. I had just had a bout of jaundice and they must have thought that two weeks in a sunny climate would help me to recover. I had started first grade in April but school did not resume after the summer vacation until October. I have vivid memories of episodes in what was a wonderful adventure for me and what turned out to be a life-changing event for us all. We took a sleeper from Berlin, where we lived, to Bolzano in northern Italy, and in the dining car at breakfast my father gave me a pocket watch so that I could check whether the train was keeping on schedule. Trains, schedules, times, and dates always ran through my mind. I recall meals in Italy—crisp roll with Italian cheese at a grocery in Bolzano, fresh fruit and cheese at the end of every dinner at the hotel where we stayed in Riva—swimming in Lake Garda, feeling comfortable in the water having just passed my swimming test in Germany, and walking with my parents along trails in the Italian Alps.

In the middle of our time in Italy, the Nazi government promulgated a decree that alarmed my parents more than any previous act of discrimination against Jews. At a Nazi party rally in Nuremberg, which has remained memorable in the history of the time, a set of racial decrees was adopted that deprived Jews of their German citizenship and, adding

CHAPTER ONE

insult to injury, made it illegal for them to employ non-Jewish help in their households. We had a live-in maid who was not Jewish, and who was all but a member of the family. My mother told me years later that reading the newspaper report of these decrees from a distance made the news more shocking and more unbelievable than if it had come in the routine of reading it in the morning newspaper at home. My only relevant recollection of this event was that on the morning after we arrived back in Berlin after an overnight train trip, sitting at breakfast in my grandmother's apartment, my mother almost immediately said to my grandmother that she did not intend to stay in Germany "even one hour longer than necessary." She said it in a tone that startled me, sounding important and decisive. Since we had just gotten home from Italy, I could not understand why we were about to leave again. My next recollection is standing in our empty apartment twelve weeks later with my five-year-old sister, parents, and grandmother, getting a marzipan pig from my parents, a symbol of good luck. By then my sister and I had been moved into my grandmother's small apartment, around the corner from where we had lived, I was back in school, and my parents were off to America, assuring us that we would follow as soon they had found a place to live. I don't recall feeling at all worried. I loved my grandmother, I loved school, and I loved marzipan.

In the year after Hitler was appointed Chancellor of Germany on January 30, 1933, about 40,000 of the half million Jews who lived in Germany left the country immediately, my great-uncle, Ernst Cassirer and his wife among them. "People like us have no future in this country," he wrote his wife from a lecture trip, deciding to give up his professorship at the University of Hamburg to look for a faculty position in another country. But my parents had no thought of leaving. They were among the many Jews who, after the initial shock of Hitler's appointment, thought they could ride out the successive waves of discrimination by the Nazi government. Many people believed that the Hitler administration was an aberration that would last no longer than the unstable cabinets that had come and gone in Germany since the beginning of the depression in 1929.

I have only a few recollections of discrimination in my final months in Germany, none that seemed disturbing. I was no longer allowed to swim in the lake where I had learned to swim although my mother, with her typical defiance, had insisted that I be allowed in one more time so that I could pass my swimming test. In the neighborhood park where we played, there were suddenly signs designating separate benches where Jews could sit. I remember a vague sense of the tension my parents must have felt, but it was not worrisome to the seven-year-old boy that I was. My parents told me later that they started me in a private school because they believed that in the public school, which my cousins attended, I might be bullied. I had long been looking forward to starting school and had no idea of alternative schools. I learned much later that my grandmother, who had lived in a Berlin suburb, had been frightened one day by the appearance of two uniformed Nazis at her door asking to see her daughter. So, apparently alarmed about what was happening in the country, she decided she did not want to live so far from my parents and had moved to a two-room apartment around the corner from us in the city. All I knew was that I was glad that I could see her more often.

I have just a few pictures in my mind of the background events of that time in Berlin. On national holidays many people flew swastikas from their apartments, but we flew the traditional German flag. There were often parades with marchers in Nazi brown shirt uniforms. I recall a day of celebration, after the referendum in 1935 that returned the Saar province from France to Germany, and I remember happily singing a patriotic song in the street. Whatever my parents may have felt, they did not tell me not to join in the celebration. With my friends I excitedly anticipated the coming summer's Olympics, which were to take place in a familiar stadium in the Berlin suburbs.

After the first wave of Jewish emigration following Hitler's appointment as chancellor, Jewish emigration continued year by year, but only at the rate of about 25,000 annually. My father had been a World War I veteran with four years of service as a front-line medic. He was wounded in the last year of the war and had received the Iron Cross for bravery. He was a proud German patriot. Losing his citizenship in September 1935 was the decisive event that changed both my parents' minds about remaining in Germany. My father angrily felt betrayed. He said he would not live in a country where he could not be a citizen, a principle that other members of our family did not appreciate until the Nazi government took one step after another to oppress those they had made stateless. Jewish physicians had been increasingly excluded from access to patients covered under the government's extensive health insurance program, and this may have threatened my father's ability to earn a living in the medical practice he had opened in 1929. But it was the loss of citizenship that determined my parents. They had heard that the state of New York honored German medical licenses but that after January 1, 1936, immigrant physicians might have to pass new examinations to be accredited. That led them to try to arrive in America before the end of the year. They therefore left Germany less than three months after we had returned from our vacation in Italy. In that short interval they had packed up all our belongings, put them in storage for later shipment to America, and left my sister and me with my grandmother until they could settle in New York, learn English, and begin medical practice.

The continuation of my life in Berlin seemed to me entirely normal and enjoyable, since I was never a child who felt homesick for his parents. I continued in school, was promoted to second grade in April, and have fond memories of living with my sister and my "Omy" in her small apartment. We were often among one or another of the many relatives who had stayed in Berlin. My only contact with my parents consisted of their replies to my very occasional first grader's letters. My sister and I had immigration visas valid for three months from the time my parents left, which would permit us to follow them to America when they were ready to have us. But after three months my parents had not yet passed the English language exams that were required for practicing medicine. They were attending night school and, preoccupied with getting started in America, they let our visas lapse. I vaguely recall sitting in the American consul's office in Berlin with my grandmother, several months later, applying for a renewal of the visas. When the consul seemed to drag his feet, asking my grandmother why my parents had let our visas lapse, I heard my grandmother say that surely the American embassy would not prevent children from rejoining their parents. That was probably my only anxious moment.

When we had received reissued visas, my parents immediately decided it was time for us to join them. Without having painfully missed them, I did look forward to seeing them again in New York and particularly to seeing New York. I had a photo album of the skyline and knew the names of the major skyscrapers. My grandmother had hired a twice-a-week language tutor from whom we learned a few words of English. She took me to some English-language movies where I was absolutely captivated by Shirley Temple in the film *Curly Top* and by a Mickey Mouse cartoon. A relative assured me that I could meet Shirley Temple in America, and I was seriously disappointed when I got to New York and learned that she lived in Hollywood three thousand miles away.

On June 2, 1936, my sister and I, accompanied by my grandmother and my Uncle Hans, left Berlin on an overnight boat train for London, to which my uncle and his family had emigrated at the same time as my parents had left for New York. He had come back to Berlin to accompany us. Twenty members of our extended family saw us off at the train station and gave us the kind of presents one would give to children going on a trip. An aunt gave me a diary in which to keep a day-by-day account of the adventure she said I was undertaking. She wrote in it that she hoped my sister and I would not forget her because she loved us so much. In childish block letters I used the diary mainly to enter times of arrival and departure at the places to which we travelled. I also listed in it the good-bye presents we had been given: candy, cookies, film for my box camera, stationery, a fountain pen, an inflatable globe, and a flashlight. A great-uncle gave me a large box of chocolates, telling me that he had heard that American candy was not very good, a comment I found a bit disturbing. As the following years brought increasing peril for Jews in Nazi Germany, more and more members of our family decided to emigrate and so we saw most of those who had seen us off in Berlin again in New York.

We stayed in London for three days at my uncle and aunt's apartment, I saw my cousins again and my great-uncle, Ernst Cassirer, who had meanwhile obtained a temporary professorship at Oxford. We waited for my mother, who was coming from New York to pick us up for the trip to the United States. When she arrived I remember thinking that she looked exactly as I remembered her. Perhaps I had wondered whether I had forgotten what she looked like. On June 7th my sister, mother, and I sailed on the impressively huge German liner the *Bremen*. Since emigrants were compelled to exchange German for American currency at

CHAPTER ONE

a punitive rate by which they lost two-thirds of its value, my parents bought as much as they could in German currency before they left, including our trans-Atlantic passage and clothes for us in increasing sizes to keep us clothed — to our eventual chagrin — for years to come. I loved the five-day trans-Atlantic trip. I wrote in my diary that the ocean was very calm. In the dining room the first morning, my mother suggested that I try corn flakes because that is what children in America ate for breakfast. That seemed like a strange substitute for German breakfast rolls. I looked forward to the mid-morning snacks the ship provided, and I loved looking out at the endless ocean that stretched to the horizon on all sides. I was allowed to go to the movies and remember trying to understand what was going on in *Broadway Melodies of 1936*.

We arrived on June 12, 1936, and there we were reunited with my father. We missed seeing the Statue of Liberty on the foggy morning of our arrival, and as we pulled into pier 84 on the Hudson River my mother held us scarily on the ship railing so Daddy would see us arriving. My diary contains the laconic entry that Daddy was at the pier and again I wrote — just as I had a week earlier when I saw my mother again — that he looked just as I had remembered him. When I think back on that time I reflect that I did not feel that my life was being dislocated but rather that I was having an exciting adventure.

We took a taxi with our luggage, crossed Broadway which I recalled from the movie, and settled for two weeks in a small hotel on East 40th Street. I shared a room with my Uncle Fritz, whose loud snoring kept waking me up. My uncle was living in that hotel, just two blocks from the small office where he had started a business importing photoelectric cells from Germany. That was to become a very successful business manufacturing electrical measuring instruments, a business where he eventually employed many members of our family, and in which he later gave me summer jobs hoping I might become interested in working for him there.

During our first two weeks in New York, we ate at cafeterias in the neighborhood, baffled by most of the choices, and at Chock Full o' Nuts, which had much less choice but strange and wonderful date-nut sandwiches with nutted cream cheese, satisfying my love of sweets. We also ate at the Horn and Hardart "automat," another exotic eating establishment where the first step was to get a handful of nickels, which you used to gain access to food displayed in glassed compartments that opened with the deposit of the requisite number of coins. New York was every bit as wonderful as I had anticipated.

My uncle was an engineer who had spent twelve years in America off and on, ever since he had finished his university education in Germany. He had gotten a job at the American Locomotive Company in Schenectady. There he struck up a friendship with an American couple who were to play a role in introducing my sister and me, as well as my parents, to life in America. My uncle was the family expert on the new country. He had tried vainly to discourage my parents from immigrating, afraid they could not support themselves in America in the midst of the severe depression of the 1930s. But once they had come he was very helpful. He had selected a used car for my parents, a 1929 Model A Ford, in which we set out at the end of June on a new adventure—two months in a summer camp. My mother and sister were at one camp, my father and I at another, five miles apart, on the Belgrade Lakes near Waterville, Maine. My parents had gotten jobs as camp doctors, which enabled the four of us to be out of the hot city and provided us with room and board while we did not yet have an apartment in New York. The 500 mile drive to camp acquainted us with New England roads and with overnights at roadside cabins. We took three days to get there. My diary entries mainly read like a travel log, noting miles traveled, gasoline consumed, stops for meals, and places we stayed overnight.

For me this was a summer of learning English along with the customs and habits of American children. I was in the youngest age group, called the buffalos, and much of what went on was a complete mystery to me. My fellow campers thought nothing of not finishing everything on their plates, a minor crime in my family. They occasionally made fun of my accent. They knew how to play baseball, a game I did not understand. And they looked forward to "color war," gray versus gold, an end-of-summer competition, which sounded scary. Occasionally my father and I were allowed to spend an afternoon with my mother and sister, usually at some ice cream parlor. My diary notes (in German) that I played tennis, went swimming and rowing, got to see plays, and that every one of the seventy-six campers were my friends. All of that was undoubtedly an exaggeration, but I was always inclined to put a positive spin on things. The camp was in a beautiful setting, about a dozen cabins arranged in a semicircle around a large grass area, facing a lake. A big bell in the middle of the lawn was rung by a counselor when it was time for meals in the canteen. When hunger struck me, I would stand there waiting to be told that I could ring the bell. My entries repeatedly state that things look beautiful and are wonderful. But I also recall feeling intimidated by most sports and feeling very much an outsider.

After summer camp my sister and I experienced a second stage of Americanization. My parents had not yet rented an apartment in New York, and so they left us in Schenectady with my uncle's friends Edna ("Eddy") and Lewi Tonks and their three children. They lived in a large, beautiful house, which Lewi had designed, on twenty-eight acres of land five miles outside the city. He was a physicist working at the General Electric company, a cheerful, professorial type of person with whom I could talk about my interests in science. Eddy was a vivacious, idealistic, civic-minded woman who swept us up into her family. Much of what we ate Eddy cooked from scratch, including bread, fruits and vegetables (often from her large garden), cookies and cake. She had a full range of electric kitchen appliances. Her Mixmaster fascinated me, especially when Eddy used it magically to produce mayonnaise from an egg and olive oil. I have always loved mayonnaise. Life in the Tonks family was exposure to suburban American life, to strange food that we ate from pewter plates, to campfires where we toasted marshmallows, to weekly grocery shopping at a co-op in the city, and to occasional stops at an ice cream parlor, where we got either single- or double-dip cones of such unfamiliar flavors as butter pecan and coffee. Neither Eddy nor Lewi were at all like our parents, and my sister asked me on one of the first days whether I liked being there. I said that I did and she said, unconvincingly, that she liked it too.

No one in that family knew more than a few random words of German, so my sister and I had a strong incentive to improve our English. And language learning is easy at that age, since memory for vocabulary is strong and there is still a surprising ability to imitate pronunciation without a foreign accent. That ability deteriorates rapidly after age ten. The members of our family who came to America in their teen years or later could never overcome their German accents, and my sister and I were proud that we could soon pass as American by the way we talked. In that setting we attended our first American school, walking up a quarter-mile unpaved country road to the school bus each morning, with Mary-Lew, Bruce, and Joan Tonks, aged 13, 10, and 8. I shared a room with Bruce, who acted as a bit of an indulgent older brother, and my sister shared a room with Joan on whom I developed a crush and from whom I learned the word girlfriend.

At the end of September my uncle came to take us by train to New York, to the beautiful, sunny apartment my parents had found. There, to our delight, were all of our belongings, our toys, our furniture, and all the familiar surroundings of our Berlin apartment. Seeing them again made us realize we had missed our things. Suddenly we felt we were home again. We had new beds that folded lengthwise against the wall, which my parents had thoughtfully purchased in Germany anticipating that we would share a room in a small apartment. My sister had a doll corner at one end of the room, and in the other I had a new school desk my parents had bought before they left Berlin. Now the travels of immigration were over. Our new life in New York began.

Developing a medical practice in New York in the midst of the severe depression was an agonizingly slow process for my father. My mother, who had a medical degree but no previous experience practicing medicine, undertook to develop a medical practice of her own, sharing my father's office and specializing in pediatrics. Both of our parents assumed positions in New York hospitals—my mother at the New York Infirmary for Women and Children, my father at the prestigious Lenox Hill and Mount Sinai hospitals. In these unpaid positions physicians made rounds seeing patients on wards and in return this gave them the right to have their private patients there. But to begin with, neither of our parents had more than a scattering of private patients—my father's being mostly fellow immigrants who had difficulty paying even his modest fees, my mother's gradually referred to her by Dr. Ruth Bakwin, the head of the Pediatrics Division in the New York Infirmary. Ruth knew of my Cassirer grandfather, a noted Berlin neurologist who had died ten years before we came to America, and she suggested that my mother use her maiden name, Cassirer, in her profession, because of her father's

CHAPTER ONE

wide reputation. The Bakwins had bought paintings from a cousin of my grandfather's who was a noted art dealer. Through these connections the Bakwins befriended us and invited us occasionally to their townhouse and their country home outside New York. I concluded that they were rich when I saw a cabinet at their house that was full of bottles of Coca Cola, which had quickly become my favorite—and rare—American treat.

With few patients to see, my father had time to be more of a caregiver for my sister and me than he had been in Berlin. He drove us to school every morning, came to have my lunchbox sandwich with me in Central Park a block from school each noon, and then took my sister home from her shorter school day. I was given a test to determine my placement in school. Since I already knew multiplication and division, I was put in a third grade rapid advance class although I had had only fourteen months of school in Germany. On my first day in school, I had no idea what was going on. I remember copying an answer to an arithmetic exercise from the girl next to me, because I had not understood what we were supposed to do on a test. This was my only correct answer, which, to my embarrassment, gave me a grade of 20%. Just then there was some commotion as one boy with the strange-sounding (to me) name of Shepard, broke a china vase over another boy's head and was about to be punished.

That drama made me forget my embarrassing arithmetic grade. It did not take me long to become acclimated to life in an American public school. The only real problem I had was that I was the fourth shortest boy in our class of thirty. Each morning before we marched into our classroom we lined up "in size places" along a wall in the P.S. 6 schoolyard so that I was constantly reminded that I was relatively little. Despite this shortcoming, a kid whose name I understood as Mcliverty admitted me to his "gang," which raced around the schoolyard at recess in vague competition with another, more prestigious gang. By midyear I was already in fourth grade, and as I became more proficient in English my grades in school went from good to very good to excellent. I can't exactly remember when I was allowed to walk home from school by myself, ten city blocks, but I can't remember ever being picked up by a parent.

Our third-floor apartment faced 79th Street, a relatively noisy cross-town bus route, across from the Democratic Party's "Cherokee Club." We moved into the apartment at the beginning of the final month of the 1936 presidential campaign and a large electric sign saying "Roosevelt-Garner" on the club's balcony shone into our window at night. I remember thinking that I had not realized that Roosevelt's last name was Garner. (John Garner was the Democratic vice-presidential candidate.) With all our family regarding Roosevelt as their hero, I had my first brush with American politics. On election night my parents went downtown to Rockefeller Center, where a large map of the forty-eight states had been erected. They told me the next morning that as the returns came in, a green bulb would be lit for states carried by Roosevelt and a red light for states carried by Landon. My father said, with obvious satisfaction, that at the end of the evening the entire map had green lights with only two exceptions. That is my recollection of the Roosevelt landslide of 1936 and my first awareness of American politics.

As a little boy in Germany I had always liked trains and train schedules, so when I came to America I had made a project of learning the New York City bus and subway systems. Getting far and fast through the city by traveling underground fascinated me, and I especially loved the subways, a love that has never left me. I knew the different routes, which trains made local stops and which speeded by them to express stations, and how to maximize how far one could get on the basic nickel fare. My parents soon regarded me as the family expert on the subway system. Month by month new cohorts of refugees from Germany would arrive: family, friends, and colleagues of my parents. My parents often suggested that I accompany the newcomers as they tried to acquaint themselves with their new surroundings and I was proud to show that I knew my way around.

My mother's enthusiasm for everything American and my father's principled rejection of everything he regarded as typically German accelerated our Americanization. Though we continued to speak German at home, we spoke English outside. My knowledge of the language quickly exceeded my father's so that he often turned to me with questions about English grammar and vocabulary. My biggest problems that first year were the German clothes my parents had brought along for me. I had endless pairs of shorts while most boys wore knickers; my buttoned shirts were not adaptable to wearing a tie; and my cloth coat contrasted with other boys' leather jackets and rubberized raincoats. I was very anxious to be American and so I was embarrassed by the German clothes that I did not outgrow quickly enough to suit me. But in other respects I had found my way around New York so well and had begun to do so well in school that I had left the world from which I had come far behind. Asked by a friend at the end of my first school year where I came from, I supposedly said that while I had been born in New York, I thought my parents "came from the other side."

2

By Subway to the World of Tomorrow

My tenth birthday on October 2, 1938, turned out to be important in many ways. Always interested in numbers, I made much of the fact that it would probably be the only birthday in my life on which I could add a digit to my age. I expected and I received a special celebration. Among my presents, generous for that time, were some real American clothes: a rubberized raincoat from my parents and a leather jacket from my Uncle Fritz, both offering me welcome escape from being teased by my friends for wearing German clothes. I also got chess pieces, an alarm clock, and what was for me the extravagance of a six-pack of Coca Cola. And I could look forward to the opening in six months of the New York World's Fair, which I had been reading about, it seemed, forever.

The day of my tenth birthday was special for even more significant reasons. Our whole family could relax because the war that had seemed imminent throughout the preceding month had been averted two days earlier by the infamous Munich Pact, which brought the term appeasement into the vocabulary of politics. The pact signed by Britain, France, Germany and Italy avoided war for the moment by acceding to Hitler's determination to annex the German-speaking part of Czechoslovakia, by force if necessary, against the will of the Czech government. My parents had been preoccupied with helping to settle successive waves of relatives and friends who had finally decided to immigrate to New York. My mother in particular was terribly worried about how a European war, which she anticipated as certain in the near future, would affect my grandmother, my aunt and uncle, and my cousins. They were in London, exposed to the danger of possible air attacks and of a possible German occupation. From conversations at our dinner table and from the newspapers that I was now looking at regularly, I was aware that everyone around me had a foreboding of war. My parents talked about the extent to which Jews in Germany were being put into concentration camps. I sensed my parents' and my relatives' deep apprehensions. Five weeks after the Munich Pact, the German government authorized Nazi storm troopers to trash Jewish synagogues and businesses throughout Germany in what was called "Kristallnacht," the night of broken glass. At the same time 30,000 Jews were sent to concentration camps. In March 1939 Hitler occupied the remainder of Czechoslovakia. In April the Spanish Civil War ended with the victory of the fascist rebel armies.

The most direct impact of these events on me was the increasingly frequent arrival of relatives from Germany whom my parents would put up for a week or so while they helped them find a place to live. The newly arrived grown-ups would camp out on air mattresses in our living room and their children would share my sister's and my bedroom. To the extent that I sensed my parents' concerns, I felt I was a participant in grown-up problems. And to the extent that my parents had no time to worry about me, they cut me a great deal of slack in my daily comings and goings. Since they were preoccupied with developing their medical practices and with making social contacts in their new environment, and since I apparently inspired their confidence, they left me remarkably free of adult supervision and gave me responsibility for my two-year younger sister. That created a strong bond between us. We had no baby-sitter when they went out in the evening. We were told to call the doorman of the building if we had any problems. Although my mother was always home when we came back from school, she let us play in the street after she had given us a snack. For middle class children we grew up to be remarkably independent from an early age.

I was often given the job of tour guide for new immigrants. By the time I was ten I knew the borough of Manhattan inside out and had a travel agent's knowledge of the major attractions. Almost from the moment I arrived in New York I had studied the system of public transportation in the city. My parents had confidence that I could show off the highlights of the city: the Empire State Building, Rockefeller Center, Macy's department store, Central Park, Fifth Avenue. The geometric grid on which the city was laid out was easy to master, and cheap public transportation put much of it within my reach. The city had excited me from the days I first learned the names of its skyscrapers while I was still in Germany. Now the problems of Europe were far away and my immediate horizon was the city. Apart from being the tour guide for newly arrived relatives, little by little I was also allowed to go places on my own by bus or subway. And I was allowed to go even farther. It served my parents well that they could send me off to Schenectady, 160 miles north of New York, to spend Easter week 1939 with our American friends, the Tonks family. With my sister in tow, my mother put us on a train for the four-hour trip, confident that we would get there and would be picked up. I felt very grown up.

For me, the most exciting event of 1939 was the New York World's Fair, which opened, after much advance publicity, on April 30, 1939, with a speech by President Roosevelt. I had long been reading all about it, and I had been saving my allowance to buy a book of twenty admission tickets at school. For $2 it was a bargain that I could not resist. I took it for granted that my parents would let me take the subway by myself to get there, and they did. I went for the first time two weeks after the fair opened. The trip to get there entailed a walk of five city blocks to the subway, three stops downtown on the local train, and a change to the train that went under the East River to the borough of Queens. Three-quarters of an hour from home I stood transfixed at the entrance to the fair, with a brown bag lunch, prepared to stay all day.

The New York World's Fair of 1939 was a spectacular event that later appeared in the reminiscences and novels of some eminent writers. It gave concrete form to dreams of a new world of technological wonders, "the world of tomorrow," at the very moment when the world of that day was collapsing, first in Europe and then in the United States. The fair fed my congenital optimism about the world of the future while the adventure of riding the subway to get there gave me confidence that I could explore the world without much money or much help.

The exhibits covered 1,200 acres of Flushing Meadow, which had been a partially swamped ash dump in the New York borough of Queens on Long Island. The area had been drained, manicured, and laid out with broad malls and green picnic areas. There were considerable distances among exhibit areas, and there were colorful passenger trolleys for people who did not want to walk. The fair was organized by themes: communications, food, government, production and distribution, transportation, and amusements. It was quite easy to find your way around. At the center stood the fair's pure white symbols—the 700-foot tall "trylon," a triangular pylon, next to a globe 200 feet in diameter, the "perisphere"—both visible from afar. You could ride part way up the trylon on an escalator and enter the interior of the perisphere, which had a model of a planned urban and suburban community: a "democracy." Visitors could see it from one of two moving rings that circled the exhibit. Its scale made it an extraordinary panorama.

After the first visit to the fair, I went as often as I could, anxious to use all of my twenty tickets. At least on my first visit, I apparently stayed all day because my mother reported in a letter to my grandmother in England that I had not come home till 10 at night. But if that is partly the hyperbole to which my mother was given, it must have seemed to her that I would never return from the fair. I frequently went by myself. Once I took my sister, once I took my father, and at various other times went with a friend. I went with several members of the Tonks family when they came from Schenectady to see the fair and separately I took their younger daughter, my girlfriend Joan. I also made it a part of the introduction to New York for newly arrived members of the family from Germany. My parents were at first impressed by my enthusiasm, confident that I was learning a lot, and then gradually amused by my persistence in going. Once school was over at the end of June, they were pleased that the fair always gave me something to do. They were not about to subsidize my adventures, but occasionally I got an addition to my 25-cent allowance for doing special chores. I liked to cook, apparently did it acceptably, and when I made dinner twice for the family in a single week, my mother slipped me some extra money for the fair.

Before long I wanted to supplement my 25-cent allowance on a regular basis and was on the lookout for remunerative work. The building superintendent had seen me carrying deposit bottles back to the store down the street for my mother and asked me whether I would do that for him. I could carry twelve quart bottles at a time in two sacks, which netted 60 cents in deposits, and I decided I would ask him for ten percent of that amount. In an afternoon I found I could make six or seven trips, for him and for other people in the building, and earn 40 or 50 cents. Later that summer, a friend from school told me that the distributor of Curtis Publications paid school boys one and a half cents for each copy they sold of their weekly magazine, *The Saturday Evening Post*, at the 5-cent cover price. I signed up for what I regarded as "a real job" after my parents had become reconciled to the enterprise. My father had at first worried that having a son selling magazines in the streets would make it seem that he was not able to support his family as a physician. But my mother persuaded him that in America many famous businessmen had started out as newsboys. An agent brought a pile of copies to our apartment every Tuesday and I would sell them in stores in the neighborhood every Wednesday after school. Pretty quickly I found I could sell twenty-five or thirty copies in an afternoon by amusing store owners with my sales pitch, based on scanning the magazine's contents and being prepared to explain how interesting they would find the issue. Most store owners were quite prepared to shell out a nickel, but they first liked to put me through the paces of my sales pitch. That turned out to be a steady source of income. This, plus my earnings from my deposit bottle business, paid for my World's Fair excursions with enough left over to put in my school savings account. My first big purchase from savings was a $10 table radio that fall, which I loved having in my room to hear music and news.

So I had the means for my frequent forays to the fair, which were not in any case very expensive. I had my prepaid admission tickets, the subway to get there cost just a nickel each way, and I brought my lunch in a brown paper bag because food at the fair was expensive. I was annoyed that a Coke and a hot dog each cost a dime, twice what they cost at a stand in the city. I always stopped at the exhibits of the major food companies because many of them offered free samples. Imprinted on me forever by repeated visits to the Nabisco building was how their chocolate wafers could be made into a cake roll with whipped cream. After each demonstration they gave out small samples. At the Sealtest exhibit I saw how machines churned ice cream and I could again get a free sample. "Standard Brands" gave out little cups of "Royal" pudding. At the Wonder Bread building I watched how dough was kneaded by huge machines. Most food samples were small and some were not very nourishing, such as the pickles at the building devoted to "Heinz 57 Varieties."

Beyond sampling food I spent time in the national pavilion of the United States, which had a wonderful movie about American history, and at the Soviet Union building, which had a full-scale replica of a station in the ultra-modern Moscow subway. I can vividly recall the General Electric building, which offered demonstrations of magnetism and man-made lightning; the RCA building, which demonstrated how a television camera could transmit an image from one end of a large room to a six-inch receiver at the other end; the DuPont building, where I first saw nylon being spun magically from what the exhibitor called "coal, air, and water"; and the Kodak building, which showed stunning Kodachrome slides of beautiful landscapes, a revelation in an age of black-and-white photography. At the AT&T building there was a voice synthesizer and free long-distance phone calls for those patient enough to try to win a call in an ongoing lottery. Thirty-three states of the United States had exhibits, as did most of the major countries of the world except Germany, and China, then largely occupied by Japan.

I loved the modern architecture of the buildings and the "lagoon of nations" with its fountains, surrounded by the buildings of many of the major countries including the United States. The fair acquainted me with the names of some of the great sculptors, designers, and architects of the period—Max Abramovitz, Alexander Calder, Jo Davidson, Rockwell Kent, Raymond Loewy, Skidmore and Owens—names I would continue to encounter later in my life.

Going to the fair on my own taught me how to stretch my limited budget and how to measure up to my parents' confidence that the fair was educational. Although I would not have admitted it to anyone, it also taught me that there were diminishing returns in the enjoyment of anything in excessive supply, like twenty admissions to even the world's greatest fair. By autumn my visits to the fair were devoted to seeing just one exhibit per visit. I chose those I had earlier postponed seeing because they were so popular that they required waiting in line for as much as two hours to get in. The most famous and unforgettable example was the General Motors "futurama," a 3,600-square-foot model of the highway world of the future, with seven-lane highways dotted with cars which, you were told, sped along at 100 miles an hour. You saw it from one of 600 moving chairs that circled the exhibit, each chair with its own loudspeaker. The model highways fed into a planned urban intersection, life-size, through which one walked at the end of the tour. In later life driving on interstate highways often reminded me of the "world of tomorrow" that I first saw as a 10-year-old courtesy of General Motors.

Many visitors loved best the amusement area in the fair: Billy Rose's Aquacade, which made Esther Williams famous; the "parachute jump"; and Michael Todd's musical, the *Hot Mikado,* a jazz version of the Gilbert and Sullivan operetta, performed in the World's Fair 2,500-seat "Hall of Music." Many of my friends' parents went to the fair mainly to go to the amusement area and to have dinner at one or another of the restaurants in the buildings of the different countries. Most notable was the restaurant at the French pavilion, whose chef achieved such renown that he established what became a celebrated French restaurant in Manhattan after the fair closed. But those sides of the fair were out of my reach; they were far too expensive and I disparaged them as ordinary.

Two months before the fair closed, the world of the present intruded itself inescapably on that dream of tomorrow that the fair nurtured. On our first American vacation with my parents, we heard on the car radio that the long-anticipated war in Europe had begun. German troops had invaded Poland, France and Great Britain were not prepared to accept this new aggression as they had eleven months earlier at Munich, and they had declared war on Germany. The flow of refugees from Germany diminished to a trickle and my parents' concern for those still left behind grew ever greater. These events did not change my enthusiasm for my day-to-day life in New York, but they contributed to the seriousness of my interest in what was going on in the world beyond the United States.

My parents grew anxious to get me through school as fast as possible before the disruptions in Europe spread to the United States and could possibly lead to my being drafted before finishing high school. They had heard that I could skip a grade if I transferred from my elementary school to a junior high school in the neighborhood, my mother calculating that I could then graduate from high school when I was sixteen. I started in a new school just three months after my eleventh birthday, in a tough neighborhood where I was sometimes uneasy. Meanwhile my sister had heard from one of her friends about religious school at the largest Reform Temple in New York, had gone with her, and was enthusiastic. I was interested in learning more about Judaism, the religion that had led to our immigration, and my parents were glad that we both wanted to go to Sunday School. We began going each Sunday morning, walking or taking the bus with two girls who lived in our building.

So by the time the fair closed I had become more interested in the real world in which I was growing up than in the world of the "futurama." But the joy of exploring my immediate world by subway stayed with me. It made high school that much more attractive because I went to a school in the Bronx that took a forty-five-minute subway ride to get there. And the spirit of the World's Fair stayed with me also. The optimism about the world of the future that the fair conveyed had offset the terrible news from Europe in 1939 and had reinforced my enduring optimism then and perhaps ever after.

3

The World Beyond New York
Going to College

The world did not turn on my college decision in the spring of 1945, nor did it preoccupy my parents. The final phase of the war in Europe, which ended six weeks before my graduation, dominated everyone's attention and my family's with special intensity. My mother looked forward to finally having her mother in New York again after seven years of separation. My grandmother had happened to be living with the English branch of our family when the war broke out and trans-Atlantic travel became impossible. In February 1945 my mother had taken me along to Washington, D.C., to file a request for an immigration visa for my grandmother. It was my first visit to the capital and included a chance to sit in the visitors' gallery of the U.S. House of Representatives. I still recall how excited I was to see the Capitol, the familiar symbol of democratic government, as we walked out of Union Station. The newspapers had one giant headline after another in April and May of that year: the sudden death of President Roosevelt on April 12th, the convergence of Russian and American troops in the center of Germany, the fall of Berlin to the Russians, the suicide of Hitler, and the German surrender on May 8th. Meanwhile the battle against the Japanese on Iwo Jima and on one after another of the Pacific Islands suggested what a long, brutal war against Japan lay ahead.

In the context of those earth-shaking events, my par-

CHAPTER THREE

ents left me largely on my own in my college planning. They took it for granted that I would go away to college if at all possible because that had been the pattern for boys in my family in Germany. They both believed that I would not be able to do my best in the midst of the distractions of the big city and the family. By 1945 my parents had exhausted the small amount of money they had been able to bring with them to America, but they had finally developed medical practices that enabled them to make ends meet. My father hoped that he could somehow afford at least to get me started in college away from home. I remember being upset when he told me he might not be able to pay for four years of college. My mother didn't find it easy to send me off to college at sixteen years of age. "To send one's son away into the world, especially so young, is not an easy thing," she wrote to her mother. But they reconciled themselves to the fact that it would be best for me to start college immediately after high school graduation, three months before my seventeenth birthday, hoping that I could get in a year before I would likely be drafted. The United States had adopted a draft of 18- to 45-year-old men a year before it entered the war and everyone knew that the draft would continue until the war was over and perhaps beyond. By the end of the war eleven million American men served in the armed forces and since I was a healthy guy, my parents and I had every expectation that I would have to go.

I had gone to a high school specializing in science, which had been my earliest interest. As I will explain in the next chapter, though I entered high school committed to becoming a scientist, I left with an overriding interest in history and government. I had been editor of my high school newspaper, an avid reader of newspapers, and hoped for a career in journalism. My parents encouraged my interests in government and history, and my father—with some skepticism about journalism—told me that to be a good journalist I first needed to study the subjects I would be writing about. I agreed.

I narrowed my choices among possible colleges. My high school guidance counselor suggested I consider Cornell, a very popular college for New York City kids, in part because it offered New York State Regents Scholarships to applicants. My parents didn't know much about American colleges, but my father had a high regard for Cornell because its medical college was in New York City, just fifteen blocks down First

GOING TO COLLEGE

Avenue from where we lived, and it was highly reputed in the medical profession. Some of my friends applied to Harvard, but I didn't like its pretentious image. The competition for places in college was modest, as many high school graduates were immediately drafted. So I applied to Cornell, and to the City College of New York as a backup. In my Cornell application I wrote:

> When I came to the High School of Science, I had intended to become a physicist. I soon, however, became interested in governmental and economic problems. I saw that while science had given comforts, health and advancement to people, governments had . . . failed to give them social and economic security and happiness. Science is well on its way to triumph over nature but governments have not yet solved the problems of . . . people. I am interested in these problems and want to take advantage of the excellent courses at Cornell in history, government, philosophy and English, in order to learn more about them. Eventually I would like to become a teacher of these subjects and a writer.

I received the news of my admission to Cornell in March and looked forward to going away to college with terrific excitement. I had a countdown calendar on my desk, and each day posted the number of days "B.C." (Before Cornell). I graduated on June 26th, about twenty-fourth in a class of more than 400 students, and received the "Excellence in Journalism" award. I had had a respectable but not a stellar academic record. I had devoted a great deal of time to the school newspaper and to the daily subway commute, forty-five minutes each way. So I was not up there among the top students in a very bright class.

On the evening of my graduation my parents, sister, Uncle Fritz, Aunt Sylvia, and I celebrated at a Scandinavian restaurant that I loved because it had a marvelous all-you-can-eat buffet. Two days later my parents saw me off at 11 o'clock in the evening on a Greyhound bus for an overnight trip to Ithaca, trusting that I could find a place to live by myself. Freshmen couldn't live in the dorms because they were reserved for students in the army and navy training programs. My father sent me off with a check for $500. Half of it would go for the first term's tuition, which was $235 per semester (about $3,000 in current terms), the other half for living expenses. He told me to open a checking account and to let him know when I had run out of money. My mother sent me off with a pack of cigarettes, saying that she thought I was now old enough to smoke.

I arrived in downtown Ithaca at 6 o'clock in the morning with just one suitcase and set about with a list of rooms for rent to find a place to live. A trunk with my clothes, my typewriter, and my radio, would follow later via "railway express." When I see parents moving their sons or daughters into their dorm rooms nowadays with a van full of belongings, I am amazed at the contrast. I narrowed the choice of rooms to two alternatives, both in "college town" near the campus, one attractively modern, owned by a young family with a baby, the other in an older house. I chose the older one, at half the rent of the first, proud of my frugality. The room was upstairs in a white frame house, occupied by what seemed to me to be an elderly couple (probably people in their 50s) and their daughter (probably in her 30s). The room was small but had two corner windows. There was a shared bathroom down a small hall. The arrangement was that I could keep a bit of food in the refrigerator. I signed a four-month lease, covering the first term, at a rent of $4.50 a week payable a month in advance, plus $0.25 a month for the use of electricity. The equivalent in today's terms would be about $60.

Only two of the five courses I chose for my first term were required. Cornell had not yet adopted the general education requirements developed at Harvard. I did have to take freshman English and a science. I expected that both would be a cinch. Beyond those two required courses, I wanted to take an American history course that had sophomore standing as a prerequisite and I somehow talked the professor, a distinguished colonial historian, into letting me in. I also chose the basic American government course and a philosophy course devoted to three "philosophical classics"—Plato's *Republic*, Lucretius *On the Nature of Things*, and John Stuart Mill *On Liberty*. It was taught by a professor whom my great-uncle, Ernst Cassirer, himself a renowned philosopher, had told me to look up. It became my favorite. It had a small enrollment and was taught as a discussion. Plato's *Republic* was a wonderful introduction to the question of what constitutes an ideal state, a book and a theme to which I returned often in later years, and Mill dealt with questions of the limits of individual liberty that I had already thought about in high school. The professor who taught it had the ability to be at once encouraging and critical, and I think the fact that I was a great-nephew of a famous philosopher gave me some advance credibility in his eyes. On the other hand, freshman English turned out to be traumatic. Convinced I was an accomplished writer, I was shocked by the severe criticism I received from the T.A. in charge of my section. He found my writing full of clichés and grammatical errors and suspected me of plagiarizing the one paper on which I received an excellent grade.

As a land-grant university Cornell had a required "reserve officers training program" and I therefore had to take a weekly ROTC drill. I hated it, both because of how physically demanding it was, and because of the military propaganda, as I saw it, that the curriculum dispensed. My father wrote me that I should not argue politics with the instructor, an army captain, suggesting that he had a right to his own opinions and that it was understandable that a military officer would stress the importance of military power. Two years later, as a reporter on the *Cornell Daily Sun*, I wrote a series of articles advocating the abolition of compulsory ROTC.

I managed the money my father had given me without any problems, which is clearly what he expected. Out of the frugal environment in which I had grown up, I had learned to calibrate my spending. I applied that learning to the large sum my father had entrusted to me though it was far more money than I had ever dealt with in the days of my monthly high school allowance and the earnings from my various odd jobs. I made a budget and kept minute records of my expenses day by day. At the end of my first four weeks, I drew up an account showing that I had slightly underspent my budget, though I did not exactly feel deprived. I was eating all my meals in the student cafeteria, since I had no cooking facilities and I enjoyed the luxury of eating out. Tuition and books were the next largest items. At the end of my first month in college I received a letter awarding me a $200 New York State Regents scholarship, nearly half the cost of tuition, payable each year for four college years. I was proud and my parents were ecstatic. An article in *The New York Times* announced the scholarship winners, so friends and family called to congratulate them. Later in the summer I received another, larger scholarship which meant that nearly my entire tuition was covered. For

CHAPTER THREE

the remainder of that first year, my parents needed to pay only my living expenses.

I stayed in touch with my parents and my sister with letters we wrote back and forth just about every other day. Long-distance telephone was expensive and I only called them—for just three minutes—every other Sunday, from a phone booth since I had no phone where I lived. The letters from my parents reflected a certain amount of what we now call "hovering," urging me to get enough sleep, to eat well, to write every other day if at all possible, and to remember to write to my grandmother in England for her birthday. When my parents decided to spend their summer vacation near Ithaca in the Finger Lakes region of New York State, I was proud to show them my room, the campus, and the surroundings. But when they asked me to spend a weekend with them where they were vacationing, about an hour's bus ride away, I demurred, saying I was too busy studying. They were upset but decided that this was a sign that I really loved college.

I felt close to my grandmother, whom I missed even though I had not seen her for seven years during the war. My sister and I had stayed with her for six months after my parents left Germany in 1935, and she had visited us twice in New York. She was very interested in my start in college and wrote me thoughtful letters. She loved music, played the piano with considerable competence, read widely, and was philosophically inclined. Several of her siblings had been prominent intellectuals in Berlin, and although she belonged to a generation of women for whom a college education was not accessible, she lived in the atmosphere of a family valuing education. One paragraph in response to my birthday letter to her reflects both my interests at the time and my grandmother's confidence in me. She recounted that she had had a visit from a relative, a distinguished scholar of medieval Arabic at Oxford, who had asked her what I was studying. She wrote "I answered you intended to become a journalist. He said that is no real study. I told him that he is wrong, because I had heard that it [required] years of study. He had not heard about that." With obvious satisfaction she enclosed a clipping from the [London] *Times* in which the writer argued that in the postwar period "no field of human endeavor will call for a wider variety of powers of intellect and character than that of the men and women who report and write for the Press. Journalism and the universities should get together." Several months later my mother wrote to my grandmother that a test I had taken showed an aptitude "for legal and literary professions with emphasis on law and journalism" and she added, "for years now he has firmly resisted all attempts to influence him to undertake a different field of study, [so] he must know what he wants."

The summer of 1945 continued to be a momentous time—the defeat of Churchill in the first postwar election in Great Britain and the victory of the Labour Party, the dropping of the atomic bomb on Hiroshima, and above all the surprisingly quick end of the war against Japan. All of these events fed my interest in politics and in political science and my fascination for journalism. Politics and music were my favorite subjects of conversation, but most of my friends were captivated by psychoanalytic interpretations of human behavior and the relative validity of different psychoanalytic theories. I took a dim view of all of this, thinking that most of the theories explained very little and were self-validating. I was convinced that the world turned on politics, not on individual psychology. My grades for the first semester of college were fairly good, but my only A was in history and my lowest grade, maddeningly, was a C in English. I had a low B in government (the name for political science at Cornell) and high B's in philosophy and in chemistry. My parents were satisfied that this was a very good start but I hoped to do better.

My interest in journalism began to seem like more of a hobby than an intellectual interest. There was only a one-week break between my first and my second term in college, since I was taking three successive terms in my first year. My favorite class in my second term was an interdisciplinary course in the social sciences, taught by two young instructors—husband and wife—who had just received their Ph.D. degrees from the University of Chicago. Unlike other courses, it had no textbook but had assigned reading in a great variety of books and articles. It opened my eyes to the other social science disciplines, to anthropology, sociology, economics, as well as political science, and it continued into the spring semester. I was so taken with that course that I began to contemplate transferring to the University of Chicago, thinking I would like the interdisciplinary social science approach that these Chicago Ph.D.s emphasized in their teaching. I also liked a philosophy course in logic, and the

CHAPTER THREE

continuation of my American history course. To satisfy the language requirement easily, I took a course in German literature. My grades improved so much in my second term that I was exempted from final exams in several of my courses.

Unconstrained by general education requirements, I chose courses for the third term in that first year in college in the social sciences and philosophy, which had become the clear focus of my interests. For different reasons, two of these courses turned out to have a decisive influence on my education: a course in comparative government and one in American philosophy. The course in comparative government was taught by an Italian émigré professor, Mario Einaudi, who fascinated me. The rumor was that his father was president of the Bank of Italy. He had flashing eyes, a shock of dark hair, and a restless manner, pacing up and down as he lectured in a theatre-like auditorium, and occasionally losing us because of allusions we did not understand or because of a pronunciation we could not decipher. The net effect was charismatic. The textbook was a West Point product, written by an army colonel, hastily put together at the end of the war to take account of the postwar political landscape in Europe. Eventually Einaudi was to be the director of my Ph.D. dissertation, but of course I had no premonition of that as I began my third term in college. Graduate school was not yet on my horizon.

The second influential course was one in American philosophy that shaped my future at Cornell for an entirely different reason. The course had about forty students, and I was among the minority who would raise questions and join in discussion. That made me conspicuous to a fellow student who lived in an unusual self-governing scholarship house on campus. He mentioned me to his fellow residents in that house who invited me down for an interview. It consisted of about an hour's conversation about my political and social views, testing the depth of my knowledge and my capacity to defend my point of view. Most of the residents were veterans, on average five years older than I was. One who seemed to be a pacifist severely challenged my views, and one, a fellow New Yorker, had a severe manner but seemed to be on my wavelength.

The house, a large, masonry structure in the Frank Lloyd Wright style, had been built in 1911 and endowed by L. L. Nunn, an entrepreneur who had developed power plants in the western United States. Finding it difficult to attract workers into remote locations in the west, he had established programs that combined work and technical study for promising young men who worked for his power company. Eventually Nunn entrusted more and more responsibility for the management of the companies' property and funds to the student-employees out of his belief that education should enable young people to pursue their ideals with practical and responsible action. That belief was reflected in a junior college he established in Deep Springs, California, and in the scholarship house he built and endowed on the Cornell campus. He named it Telluride House after the Colorado town where many of his power plants were located. Nunn set up Telluride Association, whose members consisted of graduates of Deep Springs and of present and former residents of the Telluride House, and assigned it responsibility for running and maintaining the house, adopting an annual budget, and inviting students to live there. For those purposes the members of the association met in a week's annual convention. The founder had intended the house for students demonstrating "intellectual curiosity, democratic self-governance, and social responsibility." It had been closed during the war and was getting started again, with just a dozen students in the spring semester of 1946 looking forward to a full complement of thirty students by fall. Residents received full room and board scholarships. The decision on the admission of students who had been interviewed was to be made in June after the end of my first year in college at a meeting of Telluride Association.

I thought it unlikely that I would be invited and I was not at all sure that I would enjoy living in that unusual surrounding with older, unfamiliar types of people. I had become accustomed to my independence, and before leaving Ithaca for the summer, I renewed my room lease for the following year. In mid-June I received a telegram, saying that the Telluride Association meeting had voted to grant me "preferment," meaning I was invited to live in Telluride House. My parents were absolutely delighted. It meant that between my scholarships and free room and board my college would be fully paid for. My father also believed that however unfamiliar the atmosphere in Telluride House might be, it would provide a broadening experience. When I expressed hesitation, my father refused to engage in conversation. Just accept it and see whether you like it was his advice. I did and I ended up living in Telluride House for the remain-

CHAPTER THREE

der of my undergraduate years at Cornell and for the first year of graduate work.

When I returned to the Cornell campus that fall, I found myself assigned to a corner room in Telluride House, with Roy Pierce as a roommate, the tall, lanky, seemingly severe person with whom I had communicated reasonably well in the interview. The principle that Telluride followed for roommate assignments was to match people with others least like themselves. I was not quite eighteen, Roy was twenty-three, he was a veteran of the war who had served in China, and he towered over me. He had attended Deep Springs Junior College after a year in a New York City public high school and had been elected to membership in Telluride Association on graduating from Deep Springs. In all of these respects he was very senior to me, but his three years of military service meant he was still an undergraduate, entering his final undergraduate year. Our New York public school backgrounds and majors in government overlapped. But in most other respects we were very different. He gave me the impression that I was quite immature and needed to be shaped up in various ways and that he was the one to do it. Some of his approach he must have learned in the army, like turning my bed on its side to get me up in time for breakfast. But part of it was his personality. He did not suffer foolish arguments when he was twenty-three, and that never changed, even when in later life it made him appear gruff or insensitive. If rooming with Roy at Telluride was something of a challenge in my second year at Cornell, it turned out to be the beginning of a lifelong friendship in the profession we both entered, he ahead of me, and me following to some extent in his footsteps. Roy's aspirations and the intellectual atmosphere of Telluride reinforced and added solidity to my turn away from journalism and to an academic career.

Living in Telluride House with a group of students from backgrounds very different from my own provided an informal education that profoundly enhanced the education I was receiving on campus. I forgot my momentary fascination with the University of Chicago. Over my four years there, I learned to live with a succession of diverse roommates starting with Roy and later including an eccentric literature major, a Norwegian student whose English was a bit halting, and one I particularly remember who was from mainland China with whom I roomed as the Communists were taking over his country. From a high school in which most of my fellow students were from Jewish New York homes, I now lived—closely—with students from unfamiliar parts of the United States and from other countries. Many of the older students were already launched on professional careers in law, medicine, and engineering. Many were veterans, one, a conscientious objector, had driven an ambulance during the war. Their political views were on the whole more conservative than mine and they didn't hesitate to challenge me. The house had one faculty member as a resident each year, and in my first year he was a highly sophisticated Russian émigré who, in retrospect, reminded me of Vladimir Nabokov's fictional character, Pnin. There were faculty guests at Sunday dinners. The house had a public speaking program that required each resident to give a speech to all the residents each term, significantly honing my speaking skills, and the presence of faculty at dinners and parties made me more adept socially. Our conversations at meals and in the halls were always lively, peppered with one-upmanship, disparaging conventional views. From time to time the older residents complained to us newcomers that the level of conversation had deteriorated since they first came. It was an atmosphere in which one was made to feel guilty if one talked about trivialities. We ate all of our meals together, and the meals were another challenge: I recall thinking that the only meat these people ate was pork, to which I had a sort of primordial aversion.

Exposure to the house's pattern of self-governance taught me how to conduct meetings, divide work among committees, argue on my feet, and follow parliamentary procedure. One characteristic of the house setting it apart from fraternities was that alcoholic beverages were prohibited except at occasional parties where alcohol could be served if the residents had passed a resolution at the weekly house meeting by a majority vote declaring the party to be "a special occasion." There was an important distinction between those residents who had been elected to membership in Telluride Association and those who were not. Non-members aspired to election, which was presumably conferred on those who had met Nunn's expectations of "intellectual curiosity, democratic self-governance, and social responsibility." Nunn was long gone by the time I became a resident in Telluride House and later a member of the association, but his views were often cited, sometimes seriously, sometimes sarcastically. Association members were trustees of the endowment whose income was the sole source of the house's annual budget. Roy was a member of a five-person committee that met twice a year to make investment decisions, and the meetings were open to all house residents. I always attended, giving me my first insight into endowment management, a formative experience that was valuable many times in my later work in other academic institutions.

Though the world had not turned on my college decision in the spring of 1945, my own world was certainly affected forever by my choice of Cornell and by the contingent event in my first year there that led me to spend the next four of my years on that campus in Telluride House. When I began my second year in college just short of my eighteenth birthday I had already completed three terms and was a second-semester sophomore. I was living in an unfamiliar, stimulating intellectual environment with a challenging group of fellow students. Meanwhile, the whole world had turned. For the first time in my life, the world was no longer threatened by dictators and was no longer at war. Japan had surrendered unconditionally just before the end of my first term in college, and my whole family could finally feel hopeful about a peaceful future. Seven months later my grandmother had at last been able to come to America, and almost immediately my parents had driven her to see me at Cornell. It was wonderful to see her again and I was proud to show her the campus. Although I was struck by how much older she looked than I had remembered her from seven years earlier, we immediately had that same easy time talking about music and philosophy and the family as when I was young. My congenital optimism about the future seemed more justified than ever.

4

Encountering the Political Science Profession

I cannot precisely identify the moment when I first thought of becoming a political scientist. I was always interested in politics, but of course that could have become an avocation. From a very young age I was aware that politics can have a profound influence on a person's life. As a child in a refugee family, I knew that political events had driven us out of the country where I was born and where my family had lived for generations. My parents talked about politics constantly, about what was happening in Germany, about what seemed like the inevitability of war in Europe when many of our relatives were still there, and about their admiration for democracy in America and for the accomplishments of President Roosevelt and the New Deal. *The New York Times* was on our doorstep every morning, and my father brought home an evening newspaper every night. I began reading them when I was ten years old. I saved issues that reported important headline events. We heard the latest news on the radio early each morning and repeatedly in the evening, often at a station that had five minutes of news "every hour on the hour." My parents followed the news of the world from which they had escaped with special apprehension, sometimes listening to speeches by Hitler over the short wave radio, reading with disbelief how Germany overran France in six weeks. I remember my father shaking his head when he recalled his four years in the German trenches in a

33

stalemated war with France. Because I was seriously interested in world events, my parents treated me to some extent like a grown-up, interested in my reactions, allowing me my own point of view, quite willing to let me participate in the conversations that took place in gatherings of family and friends. They let me share some of their worries about the world without however shaking my sense of security.

Political news provided the context of my early teens. My high school years coincided exactly with America's participation in the Second World War and with the patriotic fervor engendered by the war. The Japanese attack on Pearl Harbor occurred three months after I started high school. The death of Roosevelt—the only president I had ever known—followed by the unconditional surrender of Germany, happened a month before my high school graduation. We knew we were living in momentous times, reminded regularly by reports of casualties that included alumni of our school, by special assemblies to sell war bonds, by campaigns to collect salvage, and by the big headlines. Part of what I wrote as editor of my high school newspaper was about political events. The unconditional surrender of Japan occurred shortly before I had completed my first term of college.

I entered high school as a burgeoning scientist and left as possibly a political journalist. At eleven or twelve I bought myself chemistry sets, did experiments, liked to talk to relatives who were in scientific occupations, was intrigued by MIT and regarded it as a college to which I would apply. Science would be my occupation, I thought, and following politics my hobby. When I was twelve my father had heard from a colleague about a new "High School of Science," which required an entrance examination for admission, setting it apart from the usual city high schools. I was excited, took the test, and passed. The school required four years of science courses. I took even more. But my childhood interest in science dissolved in the political environment of my high school years. For one thing I discovered that science was quite a different enterprise from what I had learned by using chemistry sets and experiments designed for children. I had a high school history teacher in my junior and senior years who gave my attention to current events some academic depth by explaining their historical origins. That reinforced my interest in politics. By the time I entered college I was certain I would major in government, the name given to political science at Cornell. Roy, my influential roommate in my sophomore year, was set to go to graduate school in government at Cornell. Repeatedly finding courses in government one after another interesting and absorbing, I began to wonder whether I would follow in his footsteps. I had first imagined a career of writing about politics as a journalist. My father had encouraged me every time he heard me say that but—as was typical of the way he treated me—he offset that encouragement by saying that I should "learn something first." He did not consider journalism a proper object of study. And what I wanted to study in any case was political science. I satisfied my fascination for the craft of journalism in college as editorial writer for the *Cornell Daily Sun*, in whose offices I spent far too much extracurricular time.

When I received my bachelor's degree from Cornell in February 1949, I was eager to get a more thorough grounding in political science than my undergraduate major had provided. The Government Department offered me a teaching assistantship in the graduate program carrying a stipend of $1,000 (about $9,500 in current terms), and I enrolled without considering any alternatives. I planned to get married the following year to Ina Perlstein, my sister's best friend in high school, who was in her first year as an undergraduate at Cornell. I never thought of doing graduate work elsewhere but becoming a graduate student did not yet constitute a conscious decision to enter an academic career. I was not entirely aware that an advanced degree in political science had only a few applications outside the academy though I also thought I might work in the government. I undertook to write a master's thesis on the sources of the German *Grundgesetz*, the Basic Law that West Germany had adopted a year earlier as its first postwar democratic constitution. The choice of that subject reflected one of the principal motivations behind my interest in political science: trying to understand the collapse of democracy in Germany that had determined the fate of my family in that country. My practical object was to obtain a master's degree.

The Cornell graduate program did not provide an introduction to the discipline of political science—what was later called a course in "Scope and Methods." Instead, each of the five faculty members in the department offered a seminar in his special field, the specific subject changing year by year. The faculty focused on political institutions, political parties, and political philosophy. I chose Mario Einaudi as director of my thesis, the European-educated specialist in comparative politics whose undergraduate course had fascinated me in my first year at Cornell. My roommate Roy thought he was the best scholar in the Government Department, and he was writing a doctoral dissertation under Einaudi's direction. I was a teaching assistant in Einaudi's large undergraduate course and took his seminar on postwar European constitutions.

My introduction to the broader field of political science began when I joined the American Political Science Association in my first year in graduate school at the irresistible student rate of four dollars and started receiving the *American Political Science Review*. The association's annual meeting took place in New York during Christmas week in 1949 while I was home for vacation visiting my parents. The chance to get my first look at the political science profession merely by taking the subway to the convention hotel was too good an opportunity to miss. Attending that professional meeting was probably the moment when I began to think of myself as a political scientist, the result of a series of incremental steps.

It was easy to become acquainted with the profession by being an observer at the convention because it was not as crowded or unfocused as the meetings later became. I already had my heroes among scholars whose work I had read: Herman Finer and Carl Friedrich in comparative politics, my major field; Gabriel Almond, who had written a book on the democratization of postwar Germany, the subject of the master's thesis I was writing; and Frederic A. Ogg, coauthor of the textbook we used in the large American government course of which I was a teaching assistant. As I walked through the main corridor of the hotel where the convention was being held and looked at the name tags of the people standing around, what had only been names on books suddenly became real people. Friedrich stood at one end of the registration hall of the hotel; my renowned Cornell teacher in constitutional law, Robert E. Cushman, stood at the other end — each with a crowd of students around him. Between them there were other clusters of faculty and students. Attending that national meeting expanded my horizon beyond the five-member faculty at Cornell, who until then had been my only visible examples of what it meant to be a political scientist.

ENCOUNTERING THE PROFESSION

I recall with amazement how accessible the profession was to a young apprentice in 1949. I registered for the convention at the modest fee of one dollar, obtained my name tag, and got a copy of the 48-page program, less than one-tenth as large as the program had become by the time I retired. I chose a panel to attend and listened to a set of papers on democratization in Germany because that seemed related to the master's thesis I was writing. Hearing papers given by professors whose research was familiar made me feel like a knowledgeable scholar.

The members of the association included significant political leaders, public figures, and well-known journalists as well as college and university faculty. In the corridors I was excited to see Senators Hubert Humphrey and Paul Douglas, Congressman Jacob Javits, U.N. negotiator Ralph Bunche, and Max Lerner, a noted editorial writer whose columns I had read all the way through high school. There were people I recognized as celebrities everywhere. I thought that this was the right profession for me: a combination of the academic discipline in my chosen field of study, of political journalism as the craft I admired, and of men in government, presumably engaged in applied political science. I was not yet certain about the direction my career would take, but all of the options seemed to be present in the American Political Science Association. By being at the meeting, the profession took shape for me.

While putting faces to names was one source of excitement, hearing papers on subjects I was studying was a second. Before the era of paper distribution in advance of meetings, electronically or in print, one had to attend panels to hear about current research. Most panels overflowed the rooms in which they were held, which added drama. Although the program was dominated by the profession's senior scholars from the most prestigious universities, it also included prominent politicians and government officials. It reflected a connection between government and the academic discipline of political science. This connection appealed to me. The program included one panel entitled "Palestine: Problems Resulting from the Erection of a Jewish State in an Arab World," where the participants were Ralph Bunche, who had just served as acting U.N. Mediator on Palestine, and Paul Porter, a member of the U.N. Conciliation Commission. Among the scholars and government officials who interested me most, because of the work I was doing on my master's thesis, were those who had served in the military government in Germany after the war.

There were also some good opportunities for close-up contacts with faculty at other universities. The program included informal discussions for groups of fifteen "of the younger men," each led by two senior members of the profession. I went to the one on comparative politics and got a close look at Harvard's greats: Friedrich and Finer. The mostly male gathering included only a sprinkling of women, a few of them well known, but women comprised only about five percent of the association membership then. One indication of how the meeting organizers regarded them was that the program included a "tea for women political scientists," which the report after the meeting described as "a pleasant occasion."

A month after I attended the meeting I spent a week at the Library of Congress in Washington, D.C., doing archival research for my thesis. It turned into a fairly substantial piece of scholarship, which presaged my later research on German political institutions. Without yet having a professional career path clearly in mind, I was engaged in research in political science and was becoming familiar with its professional organization. When I received my master's degree in June 1950, I was glad to be admitted to the doctoral program in the Government Department at Cornell. Without having made an explicit choice, two months before I was married I was on the way to making academic political science my occupation. The academic profession was one my parents could understand and admire and that sustained their confidence in me even at a moment when they worried that I was getting married too young.

5

Lessons in the Liberal Arts at Mount Holyoke College

Nineteen hundred fifty-three was not a good year to start an academic career. Budgets of colleges and universities had not adjusted to the rapid rise in prices and wages that occurred after the end of World War II. They had not yet adopted the later practice of raising tuition in step with inflation. Consequently they were reluctant to hire new faculty. In 1952 the Social Science Research Council had offered one-year postdoctoral research fellowships to tide over unemployed Ph.D.s until they could find positions. But that program was no longer in effect when I began to look for a job. In the face of such dismal prospects, my uncle, who had long wanted me to work in his scientific instrument company, predicted that if I persisted in my ambition to have a career as a political scientist, I would starve. But I was undeterred. My long-standing interest in politics and political science was by then deeply grounded. My college roommate had gotten a political science Ph.D. in 1950 and now held a faculty position at Smith College. A Ph.D. degree in political science had only two principal career applications: in government or in teaching. I was sure I wanted to teach and to do research. So I never had any question that I would pursue a college or a university career if I could get an academic job. I regarded a government job as second best if I had no alternative.

In January 1953 I sent out thirty letters to political science departments in the principal private colleges of the northeast, asking about the possibility of an appointment, saying something about my four-year teaching experience as a T.A. in the graduate program at Cornell University, and enclosing my modest vita. In my job search I was pretty much on my own. I had chosen Mario Einaudi, who had supervised my master's thesis, to be my Ph.D. dissertation director. A European scholar whose prospects for an academic career had been blocked by the fascist regime in his native Italy, he was not yet well connected in the political science profession in this country. In any case graduate departments did not routinely organize job searches for their students. Information about job prospects came randomly out of the friendship networks among faculty at different institutions, and each faculty member would judge whether a particular opening was suitable for a particular graduate student. There was no open recruitment, let alone affirmative action. I did not want to live more than a day's drive from New York, where my father was recovering from a stroke. I focused on private colleges because in the northeast public universities did not have the standing they achieved a decade later. My parents did nothing to discourage my ambition, although they may have worried that I could be of no help to them financially if my father's illness required it.

I did not receive a single positive response to my letters. I had not yet completed my dissertation on "The Effects of Governing on the British Labour Party." I was still writing up the results of the research I had done in Great Britain the previous summer and I was a T.A. teaching four discussion sections in the introductory courses, so my credentials were hardly impressive. But I was anxious to get a job. I was married, we were hoping to start a family, and my stipend as "Head T.A." of $1,200 (about $9,900 in current dollars) left us strapped and dependent on my wife Ina's temporary job. My dissertation director had hired her as a secretary on his research grant, a small fringe benefit in the era of favoritism.

In March Professor Einaudi returned from a lecture trip and told me with obvious pride that he had a lead for me in my job search. "Where?" I asked him. "Mount Holyoke College in South Hadley, Massachusetts," he said, identifying it only as the place where the well-known poet historian, Peter Viereck taught. I knew of Viereck. Quite by coincidence, my only written work about to be published was a critical review of Viereck's most recent book, which I wrote with the typically superior airs of a graduate student. Later I hoped that he had not seen it. Mount Holyoke had a temporary one-year opening. With my mind on a larger research college or university and on a tenure-track appointment, I asked Einaudi why I should be interested in a one-year appointment at a small college. "Because it's a job," he replied. Like all graduate students at major research universities, it was of course my expectation that I would pursue a career at a comparable institution. But at this moment I knew I had to be realistic about the alternatives. On a visit two years earlier to my former roommate, who was then at Smith College, Ina and I had driven through the nearby Mount Holyoke campus. So we had a picture of it in our minds, knew that like Smith it was a women's college, and knew also that it was in a lovely small-town, New England setting. It was not after all an unattractive prospect for what sounded like a temporary first job. In any case it was my only alternative to another year in graduate school.

In my application letter I explained my conviction that a comparative government course should not take a "country-by-country" approach but should consist of "broad and constant comparison of political institutions and currents of thought" to identify valid generalizations about politics. That was an outlook I had gotten from Einaudi, who in turn reflected the European approach to the study of politics, with its emphasis on theory and generalization. Although I did not know it at the time, I found later that this sat well with faculty at Mount Holyoke, who disdained textbooks and had convictions about teaching political science as a coherent discipline rather than as a set of courses on separate systems of government. In this teaching-oriented institution, the faculty had given far more attention to developing a coherent political science curriculum than the faculty at Cornell had. I was to learn later that the founding member of the Mount Holyoke department, a Bryn Mawr Ph.D., had published an article in the *American Political Science Review* in which she wrote that "the political scientist must decide whether he [sic] will allow his subject to be absorbed" by its neighboring fields "or will attempt to reestablish itself as a distinctive discipline." She had designed a two-semester introduction to political science that every faculty member taught. I was to learn a great deal about teaching political science at Mount Holyoke. I developed an admiration for the education that a dedicated faculty in a small liberal arts college can provide for students. That respect for liberal arts colleges never left me, even when I later spent most of my career in a large research-oriented university.

Donald Morgan, chair of the Mount Holyoke department, invited me and Ina to come for an interview. It was an experience I will never forget. Don was a gracious man, blind since adolescence, but overcoming blindness to write a notable Harvard dissertation on an early Supreme Court justice, William Johnson, "the first dissenter," which he was in the process of turning into a Harvard University Press book. He was the first person I talked to at Mount Holyoke. His spacious office, filled with books, was in the library, as were many faculty offices. Since books had to be read to him as he took notes in Braille, he employed a team of student readers. In a four-person department he was the most accomplished scholar, and we communicated with each other easily from the start. In my time at Mount Holyoke he was to publish another book on *Congress and the Constitution,* and from the start we had more in common as scholars than either of us had with the other members of the department. After a brief initial conversation he said that we needed to keep an appointment with "Mr. Ham," a name I had not heard before and thought might be a joke. I had not seen the college catalog before I came and knew precious little about the college, including that the president was a little-known literary scholar named Roswell G. Ham. We walked the short distance to the administration building, a churchlike structure in the middle of campus, Morgan led by his seeing-eye dog. Mr. Ham rose from the desk in his elegant office and shook my hand. He was a large, imposing individual who spoke in a sonorous voice. He asked me a few miscellaneous questions for about ten minutes, said that he hoped I had "private means" because unfortunately the college would not be able to offer me a salary I could live on, without specifying that further, and then turned to Professor Morgan and said, "He passes muster." I had passed the first hurdle.

No one used titles at Mount Holyoke—not "professor," not "doctor," and certainly not "president" or "dean." Everyone was either "Mr." or, of course in most instances, "Miss." Men constituted only one-third of the faculty, a proportion that had been growing for two decades as the number of women aspiring to academic careers had been in surprising decline since the 1920s, to the distress of the senior women. The use of first names came after a while, but students never addressed faculty by first name and faculty addressed students as "Miss."

After we got back to Don's office, we had a lengthy discussion about my interests in political science, courses that needed to be covered, and housing in South Hadley. Ina was included at lunch in the town's inn. It became clear that the department wanted to look her over as well as me. In the small-town environment of Mount Holyoke College, there was some concern that a new faculty member "fit in." Many of the faculty members at the college were single women, including two of the three senior members of the department, and in an unarticulated way they probably regarded hiring a married faculty member as hiring a family. In the course of our visit, it dawned on Ina and me that there might be less separation between my job and the rest of our life than we were accustomed to.

Then came my encounter with the two tenured women, whom I saw separately, my first clue to the gulf between them. Ruth Lawson, a specialist in international relations, a Mount Holyoke alumna who had been a student and protégé of the department's founder, engaged me in a lively and friendly discussion of the emerging European Union, about which she was obviously enthusiastic. My training by a European scholar sat well with her. She was eventually my principal supporter in the department. Then I met with the other senior woman faculty member, Victoria Schuck, an American government specialist and a Stanford Ph.D. who had been the previous department chair. She tested my attitude toward the "behavioral revolution" in political science, with which I was barely acquainted, and clearly viewed my "pre-behavioral" approach to the discipline skeptically. It had been the heavy enrollment in her political parties course during the presidential election the previous year that had led to the one-year instructor position for which I was being considered. There were many pauses in our conversation. I learned quickly that Vicky Schuck regarded this position as her personal fief, and I learned later that she voted against my appointment and against my tenure. For the moment I merely sensed the existence of a turf war in the department, but at first I had no idea how important that was.

The seriousness of the division in the department did not become clear until I started there. Victoria Schuck was "Vicky" to everyone ex-

CHAPTER FIVE

cept Ruth Lawson, who ostentatiously called her "Victoria," drawing out her pronunciation of the name. The two regularly exchanged testy memos and created a tense atmosphere in department meetings that Don Morgan tried quietly to mediate and which a young, untenured member, the only other man in the department, tried earnestly to escape. Each one actively recruited students to her courses with the result that students venerated and were aligned with one or the other. But at this first encounter during my interviews, these were only vague forebodings of what I might be in for and it passed over me as my hope for an appointment grew.

Ina and I hoped very much that I would get the job at Mount Holyoke. Although the department felt odd by comparison to the one in which I had been educated and although South Hadley, Massachusetts, would be a considerably unfamiliar environment for us, it was a job, for one year anyway, and staying on at Cornell as a T.A. and uncertain employment for Ina seemed a very poor alternative. That it was in New England, a region we knew and loved, and just a four-hour drive from New York, was an attraction. There was no difference between us: we were anxious to finish the graduate school phase of our life, and this was the only available route.

Two weeks after our visit to South Hadley, I received an offer: a one-year appointment as an instructor, with a salary of $3,500 (less than $30,000 in current dollars), no fringe benefits or retirement contributions, and a teaching load of three courses each semester, with a possible fourth course if enrollments required it. The subjects of the courses would be assigned later. We were both pleased and I accepted the offer.

Finding a place to live was the next odd experience. In that small New England town there were no vacancies in the few apartments and houses that the college owned and rented to faculty. In a few rambling, colonial-style houses, there were apartments for rent in curiously partitioned spaces. It was the going belief that faculty ought to live within walking distance of campus, not only for their own convenience but to make it possible for students to come to faculty at home for conferences, seminars, or just for tea. We were discouraged and felt a little claustrophobic in this small-town, small-college setting. At the end of a day of looking, we heard of an apartment "far out of town" in a house two miles away.

It turned out to be a four-room furnished apartment above an extension wing of an eighteenth-century farmhouse, with no two rooms on the same level, owned by an insurance salesman and his wife. You entered from a back garden entrance, up a long staircase, and first encountered the bathroom and a small bedroom. Then to the left and down two steps you came to a long, narrow kitchen with a window looking out on the garden, up two steps and left again came a low-ceilinged living room, and finally down a step and to the right was a sizeable, attractive knotty pine-paneled bedroom. We liked the apartment's eccentricities, we liked the rent — $75 per month (about $600 in today's dollars) — and we liked the privacy that distance from the small college town offered. We signed a lease on the spot, so quickly that by the time we got back home we had difficulty remembering the details of the rooms and closets. Ina's mother, who came up from New York to look at apartments with us, was astonished. She said later that her "heart sank" when she thought we would live there, so unlike was it from anything she — or we — had ever lived in before. But though the apartment consisted of a set of rooms that were cobbled together, it charmed us. We had few possessions, hardly any furniture, and so we had no concern about fitting our things in.

Our move to South Hadley was not simple, but we were excited by the prospect that I was trading in life as a graduate student for a regular, even if apparently temporary, faculty position. We transported all of our belongings in an open U-Haul trailer. The trailer hitch kept coming loose and the tarp over our belongings did not stay put, so it was a long, hot midsummer trip with many stops. Ina was expecting our first child, and I was still expecting to finish my dissertation. Her expectations were fulfilled more promptly than mine. Loaded with challenging courses, I did not manage to finish the dissertation till the end of the following summer, nearly six months after our first baby, Deborah, was born.

Our initial days in South Hadley had some surprises. Our landlady told us that she had taken our empty wine bottle out of the open garbage can so that her husband would not be upset that we "drank." We learned in the little South Hadley grocery that items we were accustomed to buying were not stocked there — why would anyone want to buy sour cream, the grocer asked Ina. Apart from such surprises, with which we could cope, our first acquaintance with the college community was not particularly auspicious. At a "welcome" party a faculty member from another department told me that I was unlikely to receive a reappointment. The only reason you are here, he said, somewhat enviously, is because Vicky Schuck had a large enrollment in her parties' course and that was only because of the Eisenhower election.

We turned our attention to getting settled. We bought some unpainted furniture, which we finished: an expansion table to serve as a desk and four six-foot planks arranged on bricks to serve as bookcases. Ina sewed curtains for the living room windows. Before the term began my recuperating father came for a week's visit and stayed in the small second bedroom that was to become the baby's room. For it we had bought our first major piece of furniture, a "hi-riser" sofa bed. I looked forward to the start of classes.

My teaching responsibilities were assigned and were not a subject for discussion or negotiation. I had wanted to teach the advanced comparative government seminar but was told that I would have to co-teach it with the department's young theorist because as a new instructor, "ABD" (all but dissertation), I was not qualified to teach an advanced course on my own. I accepted that arrangement. It turned out that my young colleague sat silently through most meetings of the course, not presuming to be a mentor in a field he did not know. In the first semester my "load" was to be two sections of the first half of the basic introduction to political science and my part in the advanced comparative government seminar; in the second semester I was to teach the second half of the two sections of the introductory course, an introduction to comparative government, and a section of American government—four courses with one repetition. I was disappointed that I would not have a chance to teach in my specialty and that I was wholly consigned to introductory courses. Later in my career I realized that introductory courses required more teaching experience than advanced courses, which a graduate student fresh in a specialty could more readily teach. Classes met six days a week (until noon on Saturdays), and a junior faculty member was expected to teach every day.

So I faced three courses in my first semester of teaching, four in the second, and a six-day week, but enrollment in each course was small and the total number of students was about one-hundred each term. It was a principle of the department that introductory courses should be taught as discussions, which meant that enrollment was kept between twenty-five and thirty students per section. I found that teaching a repetition of a course gave me a chance to learn from the first to the second, and I generally came out of the second having gained confidence that I was doing quite well. I was struck from the start that the students were more uniformly attentive, respectful, and conscientious about doing assignments than the average Cornell student in large introductory courses had been. Although many were excessively respectful of the teacher, some students were willing to engage in argument and discussion. That the classes were entirely composed of women seemed entirely irrelevant. What was relevant was that they were recruited largely from some of the best public schools in the northeast and in many cases came from professional families who took education seriously. Their good preparation for college and their earnestness in the classroom were my greatest satisfaction through my years there.

I spent many hours each day and usually late into the evening preparing my classes and struggling to keep one step ahead of the students. I was not given a faculty office but had a carrel in the library where I kept books and student appointments. The Introduction to Political Science turned out to be a challenge, requiring me to go back to Plato and to later political theorists as well as to international relations, fields I had left far behind. The course bore the designation "B1-B2" indicating it was basic to the discipline. Students referred to these basic courses, which existed across the disciplines, as "baby" courses, but that was not to disparage them. They were actually quite demanding, ranging across varied kinds of reading including original sources, and requiring a good deal of paper writing. I had been assigned to teach almost everything other than what I was quite well prepared for and wanted to teach.

After a lifetime of experience with the vagaries of department meetings, from the time early in my career when they reflected the clear hierarchy of rank among their members to the time in which each member claimed equal status, the Mount Holyoke meetings still stand out as particularly tense. The sharp conflicts between my two senior women colleagues seemed at any moment to be explosive. I maneuvered constantly to try to hold my own and to stay out of their way. The weekly department meeting went late into what was our accustomed dinner hour and that added to the tension I felt. So did my concern for our long-suffering department chair, who was literally blind to the angry glances of his colleagues and sometimes failed to understand what the controversies were all about.

The hostile disagreements between my colleagues came out most clearly in the months devoted to the preparation of the general examination in political science that students had to pass before graduation. Every faculty member had to contribute questions and preparation of the exam occupied several weeks of meetings. Reaching agreement on students' exam grades and, in the case of honors students, in the evaluation of their honors theses, was extremely contentious. Each of my senior women colleagues was particularly determined to demonstrate that her students were the most accomplished. I found it painful to witness these controversies. Aware of the competition among faculty, students could not avoid becoming aligned with one faculty member or the other. That seemed to me a terrible consequence of faculty competitiveness. But though I didn't realize it at the time, these departmental conflicts prepared me for contentiousness within departments about even more important issues than undergraduate grades, conflicts I encountered and had to cope with again and again in my career.

The social context of life in the Mount Holyoke community was a series of new experiences. In the first months of life in South Hadley, a succession of members of the faculty apologized that they had not called on us, apparently at one time a customary way of welcoming newcomers, leading to unexpected drop-ins that we were glad to escape. We were welcomed instead by invitations from faculty, often for potluck suppers, which had become an accepted way of entertaining. Many of my new colleagues cultivated a genteel poverty, especially those with children trying to stretch their meager salaries to support their family. We were occasionally asked in advance of a party whether there was anything we did not eat, perhaps a way of inquiring whether we kept kosher. South Hadley was an overwhelmingly Protestant community, with a Congregational church and an Episcopalian meeting house in town, which were social centers as well as religious institutions for townspeople. There were very few Jewish or Catholic faculty or students, but they did not segregate themselves. The college still required students to attend chapel several times a semester, though most students resented that. Some of the older male faculty members were a self-conscious minority, and they did engage in some self-segregation. They belonged to the first cohort of men to be appointed to what had been an entirely female faculty. They met weekly at their own lunches and occasionally had their own parties, feeling the need for male bonding. I resisted being recruited to that group. With few exceptions, I got along equally well with women as with men on the faculty, and soon had acquaintances in many departments.

Making ends meet on the meager salary that the College president had warned me about was a constant concern, but it did not surprise us and we did not suffer. Ina worked a succession of three different part-time jobs in our first year, earning just $200 in total (about $1,700 in current dollars) but usefully supplementing my salary. Translating 1953 dollars into current dollars misses the movement of different costs. Relatively speaking, food was more expensive then, so extra income significantly helped our food budget.

Our daughter Deborah was born on the day of the monthly faculty meeting seven months after our arrival in South Hadley. She arrived the day after we had attended a Phi Beta Kappa lecture at the college, which we later recalled as a sign that she would follow an academic path. We drove to the hospital in the morning. The department had one graduate student—it offered a master's degree—and I called her to take my morning class that day. But since fathers were not allowed in the delivery room, I saw no reason not to attend the afternoon faculty meeting while our baby was on the way, and when I came to the hospital late in the day she had not yet arrived. I got the news in the waiting room from a nurse who announced: "Congratulations, you have a new baby girl." I remember thinking that the implication was that having a baby was a regular event for us. But it wasn't. We had taken a few prenatal classes but when we took Deborah home we were in many ways winging it. We took her home after Ina had spent just five days in the hospital although the maternity plan allowed for seven. But five days was all she could stand on the ward in Holyoke Hospital, which we had chosen because it was the lowest cost accommodation available. Without fringe benefits, we had

CHAPTER FIVE

opted not to buy the available but expensive group hospital insurance. Right from the start Deborah was a bargain.

Fortunately she was born at the beginning of spring break, so I could be a full-time round-the-clock father for the first ten days, without parental help. In keeping with the tradition of the time, we had not bought a crib or other equipment for the spare bedroom that would be the baby's room until after the baby was born. Don Morgan's wife had given us an old, heavily used basket that I had repaired and repainted to be Deborah's first bed and a baby scale on which we checked Deborah's weight several times each day. Everything else we needed in the spare bedroom was improvised or acquired as Deborah grew. The sofa bed we had bought for my father served as a changing table. The kitchen sink served as a wash basin for the baby's clothes, which we swished around in the water with a hand-held, motor-driven paddle, on loan from Roy's wife. Ina's parents made a major contribution to our ability to cope by persuading us to get diaper service and paying for it. My parents came up to meet Deborah, and I recall my father saying, as he leaned over the basket to look at her, that the first thing she had to learn was the difference between night and day. Already quick on the uptake, she immediately began sleeping through the night.

Although I had been given only a one-year appointment, I had apparently acquitted myself well enough to receive another year's appointment for the following year, but I had made no progress on my dissertation. I was determined to finish it before the fall term began and managed to do that by persistence, working at the table in our bedroom/study through the hot summer months. I sent the manuscript to Professor Einaudi at the beginning of September hoping to be able to defend it and get my Ph.D. in January, hoping most importantly that this would lead to a third year's appointment. But I heard nothing from Einaudi for more than three months and would not have dared to write him to inquire. Two days before Christmas, just as we were leaving to spend a few days with our parents in New York, I received a special delivery letter from him. It was very brief, reflecting his hands-off approach to the supervision of my dissertation. "I am sorry it took me such a long time to let you have my conclusions about your dissertation," he wrote, and went on:

I am very happy to tell you that I have not only read it with interest but with pleasure, and that I find it entirely acceptable as it stands. It is a fine piece of research, into which you have put a great deal of painstaking documentation and serious thought.

How are we going to proceed from this point on; is there a chance that you might spend a day with me in Ithaca going over some questions of detail? When do you expect to take the final examination? Are you planning on a June degree?

Still hoping for a January degree, I was quick to reply that I would be glad to come to Ithaca in the first days of January. I went for what turned out to be just a two-hour review of what revisions the dissertation might need. Back in South Hadley I spent two hurried weeks making changes. Later that month I went to Ithaca for a second time, to defend the dissertation by the deadline for a January degree.

I went on each trip by myself, eight or nine hours by train and bus, because we were suddenly without a car. We had spent Christmas with our parents in New York and on the way back an uninsured driver plowed into us as we waited at a traffic light and totaled our car. None of us was seriously hurt but as I look back I am still appalled at how ignorant we all were about car safety at that time. Our nine-month-old daughter sat in a primitive, canvas car seat that was hooked by two plastic hangers over the front seat of our car, between Ina and me. I was propelled against the rigid steering wheel and broke a couple of ribs. The car was a total loss. We spent three hours in a gas station, waiting for Roy, whom we had phoned to ask whether he could drive down from Smith College to pick us up. We would not have dreamed of renting a car. When I received my Ph.D. three weeks later, Ina provided an elegant surprise party for me that included Roy and his wife and other friends from Smith College.

So early in 1955, even though carless for the moment, we had realized the expectations we had when we moved to South Hadley: we had started a family, I had my Ph.D. degree, and I had a good prospect of a third one-year appointment. I had a start to an academic career but it wasn't much: still an instructor, no tenure-track position, no publications. We had begun to feel at home in the small-college community in that small New England town. It was in many ways a sophisticated academic community, and the contacts my senior colleagues had at neighboring universities, in Washington, D.C., and with European scholars and political leaders—provided a sense of being a part of the profession beyond South Hadley. I rejected a job possibility at Northwestern University in Evanston, Illinois, that Einaudi had mentioned to me, which reflected both our priorities and the political atmosphere at that time. The salary would have been between $500 and $1,000 higher than my salary at Mount Holyoke but Evanston, Illinois, was just too far from our parents. A final paragraph in the letter from the chairman at Northwestern to Einaudi is an interesting sign of the times. He wrote:

> I also call your attention to the fact that this university signed the statement of the American Association of Universities eschewing communists. We shall therefore want to know the state of your confidence that any man [sic] you write about is on this side and not the other side of that big issue.

That was a reflection of the McCarthy era in American politics, which touched colleges and universities as they sought to avoid intrusion into their affairs by imposing or rejecting the imposition of loyalty oaths on their faculty. That never became an issue at Mount Holyoke, but discussions of the communist threat certainly entered many conversations, both in and out of the classroom.

Though I had a leg up on an academic career, it was clear to me that the next step was to develop a research record. Doing that in the environment of a small, teaching-oriented college, turned out to be extremely difficult. I wanted to do research in Europe, I needed a research leave but I was still on year-to-year appointment, and I needed research funds. That required difficult negotiations with my colleagues, which is the story of the next chapter.

6

Postwar Germany
Questions and Impressions

The faculty at Cornell had instilled in its graduate students the ambition to develop a strong research career but doing that at a small liberal arts college was not easy. Once I had completed my degree, my Cornell teachers were not there to give me advice, and on the Mount Holyoke faculty there were relatively few publishing scholars. We all knew that promotion and tenure in political science depended on regularly publishing articles in academic journals or on publishing a book. Our Cornell teachers set the example. My fellow graduate students, who had gotten their degrees just before me, were already publishing. But there was a conflict between my ability to extend my year-to-year appointment at Mount Holyoke and my ability to develop a scholarly reputation in the profession. The prospect of annual reappointment at the college turned on my popularity as a teacher, on the size of my enrollments. My teaching assignment was three courses each semester and occasionally a fourth.

Although I wanted to turn my research from British to German politics, the most immediate way to get some work published was to turn my dissertation on the British Labour Party into an article. I was on my own and took the obvious route, carving what I hoped would be an article out of my dissertation but without immediate success. Out of inexperience, I took everything I thought interesting in the dissertation and recast it into one long manuscript. The subject was the effects on the British Labour Party of having won a majority in Parliament for the first time in its history in 1945 and assuming responsibility for governing Britain. I submitted it to the *American Political Science Review* hoping to get some personal attention because its editor had been a former member of Telluride Association. I heard nothing for nine months and did not think it appropriate to inquire. I then received a mildly encouraging letter from the editor, enclosing four pages of handwritten notes on yellow sheets of paper with detailed advice on revisions. He wrote that my manuscript was much too long for an article, that it lacked focus, but that it contained interesting material. He suggested that I divide it into two, more-focused articles. Before the procedure of peer review had been established, the editor of the *Review* apparently made the decision on publication on his own, doing as much consultation as he deemed necessary. The comments I received were clearly his. I followed his advice, divided the article, resubmitted one part to the *Review* and the other to the *Journal of Politics*. Both were eventually accepted, and so three years after I had obtained my Ph.D. I had publications in the profession's two top journals and some confidence that my work was publishable. That was progress, but by the expectations at major universities it was slow.

Meanwhile I shifted gears and left research on British politics behind. It was a well-tilled field. The democratization of Germany, which had been the subject of my master's thesis, was not. I was interested in that subject for personal reasons, to help me understand what had happened in the country where I was born and which my family had had to leave. Since I had a childhood knowledge of German, I was confident that I could do research in primary sources. Furthermore there was considerable interest in political science on the newly adopted constitutions in postwar Europe. Einaudi had written on that subject. I thought work on some aspect of the new system of government in Germany was a promising opportunity for me.

The first step was to obtain some funding to do research in Germany and to arrange to be able to come back to Mount Holyoke. Both proved to be difficult. I had not been in Germany since my family left twenty years earlier. Though my father had bitterly said that he would never set foot in that country again, he expressly told me that he would have no objection to my doing research there. His health was precarious in these years after his stroke, but my family was not the obstacle to pursuing my research—my colleagues at Mount Holyoke were. I had received a third one-year appointment when I applied for a Fulbright research grant hoping to do research in Germany in what would be my fourth year at the college. I did not consider alternative funding opportunities. While Fulbright grants for teaching were relatively available, research Fulbrights were rare. I knew of few other sources of research support for a young scholar and the kind of advice now available on all campuses in sponsored programs offices did not exist.

This led to a series of negotiations that were frustrating at the time and still seem incredible in retrospect. When I told my chairman, Don Morgan, that I wanted to apply for a Fulbright, he told me to go ahead but said that I should realize that if I received the Fulbright for 1956–57 there was no assurance that I would have an appointment to which to return. Although he was the most scholarly of my colleagues and I thought he would encourage me, he was always uncertain in his dealings with his two tenured women colleagues and I suppose he doubted that they would support my plans. Meanwhile I was doing well as a teacher, my classes were well attended, the college budget looked better, enrollments in our courses had grown, and a new instructor had been appointed in the department. I was no longer lowest on the totem pole. I had some confidence that I would receive a promotion to assistant professor and a regular two-year appointment after my third year as an instructor and decided to take a chance on that. In spring 1956 I did indeed receive my first regular, tenure-track appointment, as an assistant professor for a two-year term beginning in 1956–57.

Things seemed to be turning out well. Late in the academic year I did receive a Fulbright award. But when I asked for a leave of absence to take up the award, Ruth Lawson, my fellow Europeanist, was the only senior colleague who was sympathetic to my plans. I was told that the department believed that my absence even for a single semester would unduly hurt its teaching program. Ruth's memo to her two senior colleagues reveals the tension between research and teaching that existed in that teaching-oriented college at that time. She wrote:

CHAPTER SIX

> We are in the business here for two purposes: to instruct and to further scholarship. If by engaging a good replacement [for Jerry] we can satisfy the first, and by aiding Jerry to get on with his extremely interesting research we can satisfy the second purpose, then we have done what an academic department is organized to do. Of course Jerry's absence would engender difficulties for us. But a department is better able to look out for itself than is an individual. I think a demonstration that we are the kind of department that is willing to make sacrifices in behalf of its members will be a credit to us in the view of our colleagues here and in the profession generally and will likewise contribute strongly to the loyalty and espirit of the members of this department.

Her memo did not persuade her colleagues. My request for a leave was rejected. So although I had previously been given only year-by-year appointments at Mount Holyoke, I had suddenly become indispensable. Without an ongoing appointment, I had been uncertain that I would have a position to which to return after going off to do research. Now that I had a two-year appointment, I could not get permission for a leave.

Fortunately one sympathetic colleague was enough to rescue my plans. Ruth, who was by then the incoming department chair, suggested that I ask for a postponement of the Fulbright to the following year with the understanding that I could then have a one-semester leave. After arduous negotiations both with the Fulbright Commission and with my colleagues, the commission renewed my grant and the department gave me an unpaid leave of absence for the first semester of the second year of my new appointment. I was able at last to take my Fulbright in the summer and fall of the academic year 1957–58. It was less than I hoped for but better than I feared.

Ina and I gave up the South Hadley apartment in which we had lived for nearly four years, the landlord let us store our belongings there, and we made plans to spend eight months in Germany. We set out on a lovely French ship, the *Flandre*, in June 1957 with our three-year-old daughter Deborah. My father, who had been ill for five years, had died ten weeks earlier, and so grief filled the weeks before our planned departure. My mother and Ina's parents viewed our departure for Europe with some apprehension. They were accustomed to having us live close by as each of them faced recurring health and occupational problems and my mother was in mourning. Our three parents waved sadly as we sailed, and we committed ourselves to stay in close touch by airmail. We did that faithfully, writing long letters often twice each week, which took only two or three days in transit, so that we often had replies within a week. Using the telephone to communicate overseas was expensive and was just not done.

Now we encountered logistical problems of living in Germany that naively we had not anticipated. We thought we could readily find a place to live after we arrived in Bonn, the small university town that had become the capital of the German Federal Republic. The Fulbright stipend included trans-Atlantic transportation only for me, and a small monthly allowance for rent and food to cover family expenses. So our resources were very limited.

Just seven years after becoming the capital of West Germany, Bonn was overrun by newly established government departments and foreign embassies and their employees. The town had not suffered extensive bomb damage in the war, but it was hardly equipped to be the capital of a large country. Immediately after our arrival, we scoured advertisements and real estate offices for an eight-month rental. Meanwhile, we rented a hotel room over a noisy bar in the center of the town. It was a large room, shared a bath with another room, and had an area we could separate a bit to help Deborah go to sleep at night while we were still up. At first we relished eating meals out at restaurants that seemed inexpensive in dollar terms. But as days went by, we worried increasingly that this temporary existence was expensive, uncomfortable, and hardly conducive to my research. I did spend time at the university that was nearby, becoming familiar with the library, while Ina and Deborah became acquainted with the parks and stores. We began to bring food into our room from neighborhood delis. Sharing one room with a three-year-old was not easy.

As we became more and more desperate to find an apartment to rent in Bonn, we accepted the offer of a real estate agent to drive us around in the rural surroundings of Bonn, where he claimed he had a place in mind. We were skeptical. He drove us on what seemed an endless ride, through the countryside and through forests whose beauty he kept ex-

CHAPTER SIX

tolling, and finally parked outside a small, sturdy looking, two-story masonry house in a village on the hills over Bonn. It was a four-year-old house, quite attractive, with a small garden. The first floor was empty and available for rent. Our realtor assured us that the landlord would furnish it for us to a standard appropriate for a professional family, as he put it. We ended up with adequate furnishings but the main room, which served as a living room/bedroom/study, had very limited adult sleeping accommodations: two narrow, hard sofas on adjacent living room walls, their flat surface shortened by upward sloping armrests at both ends. After the first night I seriously wondered whether we could survive such uncomfortable sleeping arrangements for seven months. There was a second room, suitable for Deborah, and a kitchen with a refrigerator—a rare luxury for that place and time. At the steep but unavoidable cost of one month's rent as the real estate agent's commission, we signed a seven-month lease, ignoring at the moment the provision in the lease that it could be abrogated if the house were sold to new owners. We doubted that the house could be easily sold. We were relieved to be able to settle down in an apartment that we expected to keep for the duration of our stay, but three months later we found that that was not to be.

Although we were pleased to be freed from the room over the bar, our apartment was not in Bonn but in a village on a bus route into the city. On our first evening's walk through the village, we became aware with some apprehension that we were living in a rural community that had outside water drains emptying odorous waste water into the streets. Life in our new quarters soon had its crises. The first weeks were incessantly rainy, and after one rainstorm the cellar where many of our belongings were stored began to flood. The upstairs tenants shouted to Ina in words she did not understand that the switch to the basement pump was in our apartment. Some of our belongings were soaked and the trunk in which we had brought our belongings was ruined. A visit from my English cousin Eric, who came via car-ferry in his new car, took away some of the loneliness that we felt far from our families.

I started on a regular schedule of work in the city. I set off each morning by bus, changed near the city to another bus or streetcar, and spent about six hours each day at either the university or the parliamentary library, finally getting into some research. The research plan I had prepared was very general, proposing a study of the development of the postwar West German constitution, the Basic Law. My childhood knowledge of German, while perfectly adequate for ordinary conversation, had not developed to an adult level. I spent the first months—July and August—in the university library and the library of parliament. In that way I developed familiarity with documentary archives and with technical legal language and began to have useful contacts with members of the staff of parliament. Acquiring a professional competence in the German language was a substantial challenge: it was slow going, even though I was and sounded like a native speaker. I was embarrassed when talking with faculty and graduate students at the university, or with parliamentary staff, to find my sentences coming out ungrammatically, failing to find the right words, and sometimes using the familiar form of address inappropriately.

I quickly gained access to the libraries, courtesy of a member of the university faculty to whom the Fulbright Commission had given me a letter of introduction, either unaware of or indifferent to his past. When a few weeks later I came across books he had written in the 1930s, I was astonished to find them marked up with penciled comments in the margins, obviously written by students, alluding to his Nazi past. He apparently had joined the party, justified its judicial ideology, and compromised himself thoroughly. Nevertheless, he had found it possible to rehabilitate himself after the war and now had an important faculty position at the university. He was anxious to be helpful to me and his connections proved important for my work. He gave me letters of introduction to members of the staff of the Bundestag and to the parliamentary librarian and paved the way for my work in many ways. Had I known at the outset that he had been a member of the Nazi party, I would not have wanted any contact with him. Although every inch the German professor, authoritative, status conscious, and reserved, he demonstrated a friendly collegiality. Once I knew his background, I was uneasy about our relationship. That was also true of quite a few other contacts with Germans who had lived in the Third Reich. The recognition that we were living in a country in which the horrors of the Nazi dictatorship had occurred was constantly on our minds. We could never be sure what relationship the people we encountered had had with the Nazi regime.

CHAPTER SIX

Living in Germany provoked a constant preoccupation with the Nazi past. That was inescapable in a country that was just beginning to confront the horrors of Nazism in lectures, documentary films, and magazine articles. One evening I went to a university showing of the French documentary "Nacht und Nebel" ("Night and Fog"), a graphic account showing the deportations of Jews to concentration camps and the condition of the camps at the liberation. The student audience sat in silence. The Nazi period was also brought home in many conversations with people we met, who often felt obliged to explain and justify themselves to us. The men said they had not fought the Americans but were on the Eastern Front, the women explained how they had suffered at home, "we did not know," "there was nothing one could do." Most embarrassing were the frequent expressions of philo-Semitism. We sometimes suspected that the people who were friendliest to us were trying to compensate for whatever guilt they felt about the persecution of Jews in their country. But I was also impressed by the sensitivity to the moral problems of having lived through the Nazi regime that many of our acquaintances exhibited. In the long run Germans contended with the country's Nazi past far better than did citizens of other twentieth-century totalitarian states, but in 1957 that was not clear.

At the end of the summer we decided to take a break and went off on a ten-day trip, a pleasant diversion with a surprising end. We went by train to Frankfurt and then on to Strasbourg, Mannheim, and Heidelberg. We enjoyed the famous university towns, and I arranged to have some appointments with faculty engaged in what was then a nascent field of political science. In Freiburg we rented a car and spent five days travelling in Switzerland. We grappled with alpine hiking and I often had to carry Deborah on my shoulders. Arriving back at our house outside of Bonn, we were astonished to find a multicolored house trailer parked outside. The upstairs tenants told us it belonged to gypsies to whom the house had been sold. Shocked, we called the real estate agent who had rented us the place. He reminded us of the clause stating that the lease would lapse if the house were sold. And sold it was.

The unexpected housing problems of research overseas continued. At the cost of another realtor's commission we found another rental, our third place to live, strange in its own way. It was a handsome three-room apartment on the ground floor of a modern house, trimmed with wood timbers, in an upscale neighborhood nearer to the city. The apartment's kitchen was in the basement, requiring Ina to carry groceries and meals up and down stairs. The house owner, whose apartment adjoined ours, was a severe, pretentious woman who required that she be addressed as "Fräulein Doktor." Her housekeeper lived in a small room off the kitchen and shared its use with us.

The eight months in Germany, with its many interruptions and unsettling apartment hunting, resulted in only a limited amount of systematic research at the time, but it provided a foundation for the work on German politics that occupied me for the next decade. What the noted American political scientist, Richard Fenno, later called "soaking and poking" would be a good description of what I accomplished. It gave me a sense for the way that German scholars approached the study of political phenomena, with their emphasis on the legal and historical underpinnings of political institutions. I became familiar with the German academic journals in the field and met members of the small group of German political scientists who were doing research on the new institutions of government. The months in Germany improved my ability to understand and read the language of politics as it was written and talked about in that country. I identified the best bookstores from which I then regularly ordered books to add to my library after we returned to South Hadley.

I attended two constitutional law courses during the winter semester at the university. That gave me access to the specialized law and political science library. One course was taught by a member of the Federal Constitutional Court, the other by the faculty member who had provided me with access to the university and parliamentary libraries and who was highly regarded in spite of his compromised past. Attending lectures and reading professional literature significantly improved my language competence and made me more familiar with the argot in which German scholars discussed political phenomena. I became sensitive to the way the language of a culture shapes how its speakers conceive the world. That library work and those seminars provided the material for my third published article in which I wrote of the early evolution of the postwar German parliament and what I thought were its unresolved problems.

CHAPTER SIX

Working on that subject led to my discovery that the Bundestag, alone among the institutions of the postwar German political system, had attracted almost no attention in German—or American—scholarship. Political science at that time tended to ignore legislatures outside the United States, convinced that they were weak institutions dominated by the executive branch in the parliamentary system of government. The chapter on "The Decline of Legislatures" in James Bryce's influential book on *Modern Democracies*, published in 1921, had discouraged legislative research for more than a generation.

As I realized that there had been only limited research on the Bundestag so far, even in Germany, I decided to undertake a full-scale study of this German parliament. From my research for my master's thesis on the postwar German Basic Law ten years earlier, I had concluded that the inability of the German parliament to enact budgets and legislation in the 1920s and early 1930s had led to the dangerous delegation of power to the executive branch and had contributed significantly to the collapse of democracy. I thought that the development of parliament in the new political system was probably an important determinant of the strength of democracy. So I was convinced that I was taking on a neglected and important research project. I subscribed to German newspapers and to *Das Parlament*, the weekly account of the events in the Bundestag, and read them regularly when we returned to South Hadley. The time I spent in the library of parliament gave me familiarity with its sources and established what became lasting ties with several members of the research staff. They were surprised and pleased that an American was studying their parliament while few German scholars had shown much interest. From an early point and throughout later years of my research, I received extraordinary cooperation. As I developed my research project more fully, the months I had had in Germany in my Fulbright semester helped to give me a clear focus on the questions I would try to answer by my research, on the source materials I needed, and on the persons I would have to consult. It was the rudiment of what we now call a research design.

Living in Germany gave me an understanding of the context in which German political institutions operate and convinced me that research on politics outside the United States requires living there. I had become aware of the range of attitudes toward the Nazi past among Germans who had lived through it, from those who claimed to have been uninvolved, to those who found self-justification in one way or another, to those who were devoting great effort to compensate for their or their country's guilt. From then on I followed the literature in which scholars, publicists, and novelists were confronting Nazism, as well as the writings of those who wanted to put it all behind them. These were the early years of efforts to distinguish between collective guilt and collective shame, in the words of the country's first president, Theodore Heuss, who rejected the former but accepted the latter. Not until the generation of Germans who came of age in the 1960s did Germany come to grips more fully with its past. When I began my research in 1957, I approached the study of the new German political system with skepticism that it could overcome the shortcomings of the previous institutions of government, which had failed to sustain democracy in the social and economic crises of the 1920s and 1930s. That skepticism sharpened the questions that guided my subsequent research and enabled me to detect the factors that eventually made the German parliament an impressively strong and successful democratic legislature.

I began to plan a full year's research on the Bundestag as soon as I could obtain another leave from Mount Holyoke. That occurred three years later, when I had earned tenure and a sabbatical at Mount Holyoke, and had obtained a research grant from the Rockefeller Foundation. We spent fourteen months in Germany in 1961–62, by then with two children, aged 7 and 3. This enabled me to write a book on *Parliament in the German Political System* that gave me a reputation as a legislative scholar both in the United States and in Germany. A prestigious press brought out a German translation of my book just as interest in research on parliament grew in that country, reflected in the establishment of a journal of legislative studies and an association of students and journalists concerned with parliament. Four decades later I was one of the speakers at its fortieth anniversary celebration.

My focus on the Bundestag, coming after my dissertation that had placed emphasis on the role of the British parliament in transforming the British Labour Party into a governing party, became the basis for my lifetime interest in comparing legislatures. I was forever intrigued by the

CHAPTER SIX

puzzle of how a legislature reaches—or fails to reach—collective decisions about governing and what determines whether its decisions appear or fail to appear legitimate, representative of the nation. I found that that puzzle could be resolved only by comparing how different legislatures work. That was a manifestation once again of my commitment to studying political phenomena by comparing them across political systems, the approach I had learned from Einaudi. Comparing legislatures turned out to be a specialization that had few practitioners in political science. My interest in comparative legislative research kept opening opportunities for me in research, teaching, publication, and research administration. The semester in Germany, with all the difficulties of securing it at the outset and all the difficulties as it transpired, turned out to provide a stronger basis for my research career than I could have possibly anticipated at the time.

With my mother and sister, Berlin 1931

With my sister, Marianne, in New York, c. 1940

Cornell sophomore, 1946

Celebrating my Ph.D. 1955. l to r: Win Pierce (next to me), Roy Pierce, Donald Matthews, Maggie Matthews, Ina (in front)

In my study in South Hadley after returning from Germany, 1958

Associate professor, Mount Holyoke College, 1962

Legislative research conference, University of Iowa, May 1969
1st row, l to r: Samuel C. Patterson, John E. Schwartz, Henry Valen, Malcolm E. Jewell, Mattei Dogan, Peter Gerlich
2d row, l to r: John A. Brand, Mogens Pederson, Alan Kornberg, Heinz Eulau, Hans Daalder, unidentified
3rd row, l to r: C.L. Kim, unidentified, Thomas Flinn, Gerhard Loewenberg, Pertti Pesonen, G.R. Boynton, John C. Wahlke

Dean, c. 1987

At my desk at home in Iowa City, 1998

7

Punch Cards to Computers
The New Language of Political Research

When computers began to be used for research in political science in the late 1950s, soon after I got my Ph.D., I paid little attention. I was pretty deaf to the enthusiasm of colleagues at other universities who analyzed legislative roll calls or public opinion surveys. The ability of these early computers to analyze large quantities of data fascinated them. I did not work in these fields and my graduate education had given me no training in quantitative research. My education was traditional, emphasizing the study of constitutions, institutions, political philosophy, and political history. We did study elections and public opinion, which required some competence in statistical analysis, but at Cornell that was a sideline. If anything, our teachers disparaged quantification in political science, doubtful that it could illuminate the important research questions in the field. Reading knowledge in two languages was required for the Ph.D. and the department took a dim view of the developing tendency to claim that statistics could be counted as one of the languages.

So my introduction to computers came later, after my year-long sabbatical in Germany in 1961–62, after I had done sustained research on the Bundestag. During that year I collected extensive data on the 519 members of parliament, drawn from documentary sources, the biographical directory of members, transcripts of parliamentary debates during the four-year term of the House, and electoral records. I had painstakingly recorded these data on more than one thousand 4x6 index cards and had brought back the biographical directory of the members and other parliamentary records. Back in South Hadley I found myself in a sea of data, confronting for the first time in my career the challenge of quantitative analysis. I wanted to relate the social and political backgrounds of the members to their performance in parliament without as yet a clear idea of what that relationship might reveal. The existing literature on the social background of members of European parliaments guided the approach I was taking, but the relationship between members' backgrounds and their votes and activities in parliament had not been explicitly explored. I wanted to do that with some precision, expecting that data on the individual members of the Bundestag would give me a way of understanding its aggregate characteristics as a central institution in the German political system. Such as it was, that was my theory.

A new colleague at Mount Holyoke, well trained in quantitative analysis during his recently completed graduate work at the University of North Carolina, suggested that the data I had collected could be systematically categorized and recorded on IBM punch cards. If I did that, he explained, the information could be analyzed using the counter-sorter in the newly established Amherst-Mount Holyoke Political Studies Center. I was interested. Punch cards had long been around for recording and sorting all kinds of information. As students we had used punch cards to register for courses. Businesses used them to keep and sort financial records. These rectangular cards, 7 by 13 inches, on smooth manila stock, had eighty columns with twelve punch locations in each column. Data could be recorded on the cards using a card punch operated by a keyboard much like a typewriter. Each card could therefore record up to eighty separate items of information each coded into one of twelve categories. A counter-sorter reading the punches could rapidly sort the cards by category and provide a count of the number of cards that dropped into each sorted stack.

I had no experience translating political data into numerical categories. But my colleague, who administered the Amherst-Mount

Holyoke Center, helped me draw up a codebook to assign numbers to information that was not itself numerical. It turned out that I could distinguish fifty-six items of information on each of the 519 members of the Bundestag elected in 1957, the primary subjects of my research. With our son Michael in nursery school for the first time, Ina had time to help me enter the data on coding sheets, one for each member, with fifty-six numerically coded items on each sheet. I learned the language: each of the fifty-six items could have different values from one member to another and could be treated as a variable. A key-punch operator at the Research Computing Center at the University of Massachusetts recorded the information onto cards, which were returned in boxes that could accommodate 2,000 cards each. Used cards or cards that had been mutilated in the machine were lying around everywhere—on desks, shelves, conference tables, the floor—so it was vitally important to keep the valid cards in file drawers especially made to fit them.

In 1964 after I had drafted some of the chapters for my book on the Bundestag, I spent many hot summer weeks on the top floor of the non-air-conditioned Amherst-Mount Holyoke Political Studies Center, using the counter-sorter to determine frequency distributions for my fifty-six variables. With windows wide open to catch every breeze, my hay fever acted up and bits of Kleenex often jammed the delicate counter-sorter mechanism. As the machine whirred, it could sort the deck of 519 manila-colored cards into the coded categories in less than a minute. If you sorted on religion for example, the cards for the 519 members would be sorted into two categories, Catholics and Protestants, the cards coded and punched "1" for "Catholic" falling into one pocket of the mechanism, the cards coded "2" for "Protestant" falling into another. If you proceeded to sort each of the resulting decks by party, you had a cross-tabulation of religion by party, and could present the result in a contingency table that showed the relationship between the religion of members and their party affiliation. Whatever the shortcomings of sorting on one variable at a time, the process provided a physical manifestation of the frequency distribution of each analytical item.

When I wanted to introduce control variables—which was about as far as my sophistication in statistics went at that time—rather than doing further card sorts, I made use of time I had been allocated on

CHAPTER SEVEN

an IBM 1620 computer at the Research Computing Center at the University of Massachusetts in Amherst. The computers of that generation were large, floor-to-ceiling machines, enclosed in metal closets, spinning magnetic tape on which the punch-card data were recorded. They were programmed to manipulate data according to specified statistical procedures. Electronic computers were a mystery to me. All I knew was that they relied on binary electric impulses — 0's and 1's — but how that resulted in data analysis was of course not intuitively obvious or in any way observable. I'd simply send my deck of data cards to the computing center, together with a deck of analysis cards that specified the analyses that I wanted done. Two or three days later a printout of the results came back, or occasionally the printout would indicate that I had made an error in the instruction and needed to do it over. This was batch processing, very slow by today's standards, as the limited time available on the computer was allocated among users and done in batches as each user's turn came. The results were printed on large sheets of paper that rolled out on spools. If you made a mistake, you had to repeat and wait another two or three days for your batch to proceed. It was my first introduction to what computers could accomplish, my first experience of the magic and the frustration of computer analysis of quantitative data, and it sparked my earliest interest in computer programs.

The fruits of that labor resulted in the chapters of my book on the members of the Bundestag and their activity, what political scientists called their behavior. The book contained forty-two tables, mostly reporting frequency distributions or relationships between two variables shown in contingency tables. They were an indication that I had moved in the direction of quantitative research. To traditional scholars, especially in Germany, where the book attracted particular attention, my analyses seemed a methodologically up-to-date example of legislative research. But I was aware that the work then being done in congressional research, using data on roll calls, was far more sophisticated. This prompted me to improve my knowledge of statistics and quantitative research methods and led to my lifelong interest in comparing legislative research data cross nationally and thinking about the conceptual problems that comparative research entailed.

Several years later, in 1967, I took my first course in computer programming. John Kemeny, chair of the Mathematics Department at Dartmouth, and his colleague, Thomas E. Kurtz, had developed an instructional language accessible to nonscience students for programming computers, called by the acronym BASIC (Beginner's All-purpose Symbolic Instruction Code). Instead of technical language, instructions in BASIC used ordinary language commands: "go to," "data," "print," "repeat," "if . . . then . . . else." Mount Holyoke offered a set of classes for faculty and students to introduce them to programming in BASIC, and Ina and I both took the course. In that same year the National Science Foundation offered grants for faculty at neighboring undergraduate colleges to spend a week or two on the Dartmouth campus to get hands-on experience. I received a grant and spent a week at Dartmouth learning to write a program for undergraduates that would allow them to compare election outcomes under different electoral systems. It gave students the chance to submit a distribution of votes in an imaginary election and to compare how that distribution would result in different distributions of seats in the legislature depending on whether the election was conducted in the American, the British, the German, or the French political systems. It was a very obvious way of using the calculating power of the computer to demonstrate the relationship between votes and seats. I used it in my Mount Holyoke classes and later at Iowa.

However, my work in computer programming was short-lived, superseded by the fact that programming in the social sciences was becoming the province of specialists. On the other hand, my interest in the use of computers in research and teaching kept growing. The capacity of computers to undertake a wide range of statistical analyses led to large programming organizations that made programming by individual scholars unnecessary. I was astonished when I arrived at the University of Iowa in 1969 to learn of the existence of a package of ready-made programs that made it easy to do any statistical analysis that I was capable of undertaking at that time. It was the newly developed Statistical Package for the Social Sciences (SPSS), was stored on the central university computer, and was easy to use with the help of a large, well-organized manual. The manual also contained practical introductions to important statistical procedures, which I supplemented by auditing two courses in statistics in the Sociology Department when I first came to Iowa. Constantly updated versions of SPSS, as of other early computer programs, continue to be used.

The Political Science Department at Iowa was well ahead of departments at most other colleges and universities in the use of computers, thanks to the initiative of a young faculty member, G. Robert Boynton, who like my Mount Holyoke colleague, had also received his Ph.D. at the University of North Carolina. With grants from the National Science Foundation and impressive enterprise, he had organized a computer network among Iowa colleges and universities that permitted data sharing and collaborative work. In the Iowa department, he administered a Laboratory for Political Research. It had a staff of three part-time graduate students, one each from political science, history, and computer science, and had such essential equipment as a card punch, a high-speed printer, a counter-sorter, and a card reader. A link between the card reader and the university's mainframe computer came soon after I arrived, so it was then no longer necessary to take cards to a window in the basement of the university's computing center and pick up the printout several hours later.

The Iowa experience demonstrated how the diffusion of computer savvy in political science originated in a few graduate departments in this country in the 1950s and 1960s, and spread from them first to other graduate departments in the 1970s, then more widely in the profession and a decade later into undergraduate education. The ability to analyze large sets of data encouraged data collection, first of public opinion and voting data and then of roll-call votes in legislatures. The expense of these enterprises invited the sharing of data across universities. The organization of data archives, notably the Inter-university Consortium for Political Research (ICPR) at the University of Michigan, enabled large numbers of scholars at many universities to undertake computer analysis, since the data collected in large survey projects became available for secondary analysis through membership in the consortium. That began to transform research in political science from research by scholars working in library archives or observing politics on location to scholars working in computer centers analyzing data often collected by others. As a result, the language of the natural sciences began to pervade the social science disciplines: "laboratory work," "findings," "hypotheses," "tests," "reliability and validity of measures," "statistical significance" of results. It also encouraged an emphasis on the behavior of individuals in politics, and a neglect, for a while, of the institutional context in which they acted. But a decade later there was a return to an emphasis on institutions in political research, by efforts to model their rules and procedures in logical terms. Computers proved indispensable once again, in this case for solving the complicated equations that were used to express these models.

When I came to the University of Iowa in 1969, data and instructions for their analysis were still recorded on punch cards, as I had been accustomed to doing at Mount Holyoke. Time between the submission of a "job" into the card reader and the arrival of the results on the printer varied with the hour of the day. There was therefore an advantage to working in the evenings when the turnaround time was fastest. That encouraged a small cohort of faculty and graduate students who worked evenings to collaborate, to share enthusiasms and frustrations, and to develop a special collegiality. I was glad to be a participant. It was still the age of batch processing. Soon magnetic tape replaced punch cards for recording data and instructions but immediate online access to computers was still a decade away.

My first research projects at Iowa consisted of analyses of the development of German attitudes toward the new democratic political institutions that had been established after the war. Together with Boynton, I undertook secondary analyses of existing German opinion surveys. In 1971 I was appointed to the Council of the ICPR at the University of Michigan, certainly not on the strength of my still-limited skills in data analyses, but perhaps because I had done research on non-American data and was interested in comparative research at a time when most survey research was done only with American data. Work with the scholars associated with the ICPR acquainted me with the wide range of computer applications in political science occurring at American and European universities. As I developed new research projects, they always had aspects requiring computer-assisted data analysis. When my term on the ICPR board ended in 1974, I had had a decade of experience with the use of computers in political research.

The advent of personal computers was still half a decade away, but when PCs appeared in 1979, the Iowa Department of Political Science was once again one of the first in the country to make them available to faculty. Every member of the department received a computer terminal for his office in 1980 and was given the opportunity to buy one to have at home. At a substantial cost by today's standards—about $4,000 in current terms—I bought a terminal that could be connected to the university computer using our home telephone receiver. This transformed computer usage fundamentally because it offered an escape from batch processing to online real-time processing, a dramatic improvement. At about the same time, computer programs were being devised to permit the use of computers for word processing. Very quickly computers replaced typewriters. Thus, a technology developed in engineering and the physical sciences, then applied in the social sciences, and eventually in the humanities, became an indispensable tool for research and for writing—word processing and publishing. As I followed along, never in the forefront but, thanks to younger colleagues, never too far behind, I was witness to this important development. It equipped me not only to continue to do research in the discipline, but also to apply the new technology to academic publishing, when in the mid-1970s a colleague and I founded an academic journal, which is the subject of chapter 10.

8

The Unsettling Years, 1968-69

Nineteen sixty-eight/sixty-nine were unsettling years in the academic world as well as for me professionally. After it was over, my family and I were settled in a new environment but the changes in the academic world were still playing themselves out. It was a year in which I had my first experience in college-wide administration in the midst of the worst disruptions on college campuses in my lifetime and a year in which coincidentally a series of new professional opportunities opened up in my career.

What unsettled the academic world were profound political and social changes in the United States. The first cohort of baby boomers who arrived on college and university campuses in the mid-1960s during the civil rights movement and the national controversy over the Vietnam War included many students impatient to bring about change. In many cases they made their colleges or universities the target of their dissatisfaction, regarding them as a manifestation of the establishment. Protests first occurred in 1964 in the free speech movement at the University of California at Berkeley where students defied rules against political organizing on campus. They spread then to other campuses with protests against university relationships with the federal government through research contracts. At Columbia University, students protested the university's plan to acquire land in poor neighborhoods surrounding the campus. The issues varied from one place to another, occurring intermittently throughout the 1960s, most frequently toward the end of

CHAPTER EIGHT

that decade. Often African American students protested separately from white students, focusing on issues of racial discrimination. The methods of protest included not only rallies and meetings, but also the announcement of non-negotiable demands reinforced in many instances by the occupation of both classroom and administration buildings. At Columbia, students occupied parts of the administration building including the president's office. At Cornell University, armed students occupied the student union. Mount Holyoke College did not escape these challenges. Its students claimed a role in deciding academic requirements, arguing for greater freedom of choice. They objected to most social regulations in the dormitories, notably the prohibition against the presence of men in women students' rooms, the so-called parietal rules. College administrators often did not know how to cope with such unfamiliar forms of protest. In the few instances where they called in the police, as at Columbia, or the National Guard, as at Kent State, violence erupted and exacerbated the conflict. It was in this context that I was suddenly drawn into administration at Mount Holyoke in the fall of 1968, which might have led me into a lifelong career there.

What unsettled my professional life was the result of the publication of my book on the German parliament in 1967. It gave me a reputation in the profession that led to inquiries from several universities asking whether I would consider an offer of a senior faculty position. My book was the first major work on this subject, it was well received, and it came at a time when many universities were expanding their faculties. Junior appointments alone could not build a faculty, so there was a high demand for midcareer faculty with a record of accomplishment. I had turned down a lavish offer from the University of Virginia at double my Mount Holyoke salary and with half as much teaching. Both Ina and I were invited for an interview there, but Virginia did not seem like the right fit. At the 1967 meeting of the American Political Science Association, I had met John Wahlke, a renowned legislative scholar at the University of Iowa, and he had invited me to give a lecture there, which acquainted me with that university. The lecture led the senior members of the Iowa department to be interested in developing a position for me. At the same time I was about to spend the spring semester of 1967–68 as a visiting faculty member at Cornell, just before the major protests at Columbia, Cornell, and Mount Holyoke. The Cornell visit, just as an earlier visiting appointment for a once-a-week seminar at Columbia, had the prospect of a tenure-track appointment. So had a previous summer appointment at UCLA. Ina and I expected that we would accept one or another of these new opportunities and leave Mount Holyoke, believing that we had come to a fork in our road. Ina had found the South Hadley environment increasingly confining both for her professional goals and for our family. I was certainly intrigued by the possibility of a position at a major research university, but we did not anticipate how complicated the decision to move would turn out to be.

I came back to Mount Holyoke from the visiting semester at Cornell in June 1968, just after the country had been shaken by the assassinations of Martin Luther King and Robert Kennedy, and just after the violent demonstrations at Columbia. Those events heightened the student protest movement throughout the country. At Mount Holyoke, most administrators had been approaching student demands with considerable concern but also with a willingness to consider changes in social regulations and academic requirements. They were also dealing with the growing number of minority, principally African American students whom the college had actively recruited and who felt uncomfortable in the college's unfamiliar white environment. They wanted to have their own student social center, which the college regarded as an undesirable preservation of social segregation. As chair of political science, one of the most heavily enrolled departments in the college, I knew many of the student leaders.

The college's president, Richard Glenn Gettell, whose career had been principally spent in the corporate world as an economist at *Fortune* magazine and at Texaco, found these student demands, especially those challenging dormitory rules, offensive. He alone in the administration was not willing to deal with them. At the beginning of the academic year 1967–68 he had announced that he would retire as soon as a successor could be appointed. A search for a new president was under way but it had apparently made little headway by the spring of that year. While I was still visiting at Cornell, the search committee consulted me once or twice about Cornell faculty who had been recommended as candidates. I knew both the faculty and the trustee members of the Mount Holyoke

CHAPTER EIGHT

presidential search committee. I had become acquainted with several trustees because I served on a faculty committee that regularly met with a group of them.

Although I had become a fairly prominent faculty leader in my fifteen years at Mount Holyoke and had been chair of the Political Science Department for five years, I was nevertheless astonished when three weeks after my return from Cornell I received a phone call from the trustee chair of the search committee. He asked me whether I would come to dinner with the trustee members of the committee in New York to talk about becoming the college's next president. I was quite certain that I would not be interested. I had absolutely no ambition to go into administration, let alone to become a college president, especially since it seemed that I was about to have the opportunity to obtain a faculty appointment at one of several major research universities. If my lack of interest needed reinforcement, Ina provided it by failing to look up from her desk when I told her about the phone call. Out of courtesy to the committee, I went to dinner in New York and then talked to each of the faculty members of the committee when I returned to South Hadley. But after a decent interval I wrote a letter in which I declined the invitation, with appreciation for the committee's confidence in me, explaining my commitment to continuing my career as a teacher and a researcher. That decision was right for me, and it turned out to be very right for the college as well because six months later Mount Holyoke was able to attract David Truman to assume the Mount Holyoke presidency. His reputation at Columbia had been irretrievably damaged there by his decision as provost to call in the police to quell the student uprising. An accomplished administrator and a first-rate scholar who had been in line to be Columbia's next president, Truman had stepped down as provost after the events of that spring. But for these events, he would not have been available to become Mount Holyoke's next president, an office in which he subsequently served illustriously for eight years. I had the privilege of working with him when I eventually became a member of Mount Holyoke's Board of Trustees.

But before all of that happened, Mount Holyoke experienced a series of increasingly strong student protests echoing those occurring on many other campuses. The trustees of the college, at their first meeting of the

1968–69 academic year, facing what they regarded as the most urgent student demand, were going to deal with the issue of parietals, the issue on which Gettell, who was still president, was most inflexible. Members of the administration around Gettell regarded me as a source of information about faculty views. In the weeks before the trustees' meeting I talked often with the dean of students, with the secretary of the college, the president's principal assistant and his tie to the trustees, and with other faculty. We all believed that the college needed to respond to student demands, to prove itself adaptable to change. We were apprehensive about the consequences of Gettell's intransigence and the fact that a new president had not yet been appointed. We knew the perils of confrontations with students from the events on other campuses. When at their November meeting it became clear that the trustees were not prepared to support Gettell's insistence on maintaining the status quo, he took it as a vote of no-confidence and resigned on the spot. The trustees immediately appointed the principal academic officer of the college, the academic dean, Meribeth Cameron, as acting president. One of her first decisions was to ask me to take her position as acting academic dean — effectively acting provost. I agreed and for the next seven months had my first experience in institution-wide academic administration, at a very challenging time. Although I was certain I wanted to continue my scholarly career, out of loyalty to the college I could not escape from administration for the moment.

Meribeth delegated to me responsibility for dealing with the immediate crises facing the college and freed me from responsibility for administering existing academic policy day-to-day, a responsibility she assigned to an assistant academic dean. She recognized that important policy decisions faced the college that could not be deferred, including the background question that had been raised for quite a while, of whether Mount Holyoke should become coeducational or whether it could survive as a college for women. Many single-sex institutions were becoming coeducational, and whether a separate college for women would continue to have an important role in American higher education was uncertain.

Under new leadership, the college was now willing to consider fundamental changes and to take student demands seriously. I appointed a series of ad hoc student-faculty-administration committees to make recommendations to the faculty and to the acting president on each of the major issues: a committee on what we called the multiracial community, a committee on social regulations, a committee on procedures for devising a larger role for students in making academic policy, and a fact-finding committee on coeducation. Each of these committees worked with a sense of urgency and in almost every case with a welcome open-mindedness. I attended all of their weekly meetings, usually for long evening hours. I kept the acting president informed of these committee deliberations. I also attended the meetings of the faculty committee on the curriculum, which was considering important modifications in course requirements. Because I was asked to take on all of these responsibilities seven weeks after the term had begun, I continued to teach my two courses in political science and to chair the department. A sense that important changes were occurring provided the energy to cope with long hours every day. There was support from the faculty for what we were doing, a broad consensus on the changes that were required, and some excellent student leadership especially from members of the student government association. Unlike the preceding generation of women students, a growing portion of the best students in this generation had professional ambitions and were planning to enter graduate and professional schools. Though they were dissatisfied with the status quo, they responded thoughtfully when they were taken seriously. The president of the Student Government Association had a judicious temperament that presaged her eventual career as a federal judge. Another student who organized an effort to revise the curriculum, which she called "Action on Academic Issues," eventually had a career as a professor of political science and as a college dean at three different universities.

The challenge of social change was of course not limited to campuses but existed in many wider communities. Ina had just finished a master's thesis in philosophy and had received a degree from the University of Massachusetts, the culmination of four years as a part-time graduate student. In the absence of further opportunities in philosophy, she turned her attention to the deterioration of the traditionally harmonious relations between Jews and blacks, coming out of the growing assertiveness in the African American community, typified by the slogan "Black is beautiful." To explore the issues and urge understanding in the Holyoke city community, she organized a two-day conference that took place in February at our synagogue. For the remainder of the academic year she volunteered at a community center in Holyoke but found that the conference she had arranged had not succeeded in motivating others to join her in community work.

Efforts to diversify the student population at Mount Holyoke racially had resulted in recruiting a considerable number of African American students to the campus. At the start of the academic year 1968–69 they constituted a small but, for the first time, an organized minority, quite self-conscious of the academic and social problems they faced. They established an informal Mount Holyoke Afro-American Society whose first proposal was to launch a summer program to prepare disadvantaged high school juniors and seniors for Mount Holyoke, a proposal that the faculty accepted and the trustees funded. Much more contentious was the society's demand that the college immediately establish a Black Culture Center, which expressed the student's discomfort in the predominantly white community and their desire for an escape, for social segregation. Because it seemed that this issue, and others arising from President Gettell's sudden resignation, could not be deferred, the trustees arranged a special meeting to take place in New York just one month after Meribeth Cameron's appointment as acting president. Black students insisted that they be allowed to attend this meeting to make their case for a center, challenging the rule that trustee meetings were closed. They threatened to occupy the administration building if their demand was not met. To avert what seemed like an impending confrontation, I suggested to the student leaders that they call the chair of the Board of Trustees to ask him to allow them to attend the meeting. In good faith, I did not want to undercut them by briefing the chairman that the call was coming. With spontaneous wisdom, and a degree of courtesy that reflected a noble aspect of traditional New England culture, he told them on the telephone that if they were to come to New York and invite the trustees to tea before the meeting, as he put it, he was sure all of the trustees would come and listen to the student proposal. The students would be able to argue for it face-to-face. I think the students were startled. In any case they were pleased.

CHAPTER EIGHT

Meribeth and I accompanied them by train to New York, and at their meeting the trustees decided to establish a black culture center immediately in a vacant dormitory on campus. The telephone conversation has been memorable to me forever, as a Boston financier graciously satisfied a group of anxious black students that they were being heard. The issues raised did not go away. The dormitory in which the center was established burned down two months later during the winter vacation, the trustees funded a new site, and the committee on a multiracial community then proceeded to recommend black studies courses and the appointment of a faculty member as black studies coordinator, recommendations that the faculty accepted. In responses to episodes such as these, confrontations with students on college campuses were either ignited or defused. At Mount Holyoke they simmered but were contained. It seemed to me that women students were just not as aggressive as their male counterparts on other campuses and perhaps prudence among those of us in administration helped to mediate differences.

As I sat through long, frequent meetings of the various ad hoc committees, I saw that there were few fixed positions on academic issues either among students or among faculty. Faculty quite naturally had convictions that the curriculum and course requirements needed to remain their province, though they were willing to listen to student proposals to relax requirements and to add new courses. Much more contentious was a student demand for participation in the evaluation of faculty by allowing student membership on the faculty committee on appointments, reappointments, and promotions. This the faculty adamantly resisted, without objecting to student input on faculty evaluations. That led to agreement on systematically gathering student evaluations for the committee, but that agreement did not avoid a petition signed by 900 students insisting on student membership on the promotions committee.

It became clear that agreements on issues reached within student-faculty committees would not necessarily be shared by large numbers of students who had not participated in the discussions. As students on these new joint committees began to see the complexity of the issues they were raising, it looked to students outside the committees that their leaders were being coopted by the faculty. Communication between student leaders and their constituents was much more difficult than communication between faculty members on these committees and the whole faculty. Faculty meetings tended to accept recommendations from the student-faculty committees, in part because after Gettell's resignation there was goodwill toward the new administration. But by contrast the students on the committees had a constituency of 1,800 students impatient for change.

Because curriculum questions were complicated and often required study, it was not difficult to convert substantive differences on a whole range of academic questions into procedural issues. We resolved most of these issues by agreeing to add students to the faculty committees charged with academic policy. In two important areas, relations with the Board of Trustees and academic policy, we established student committees parallel to their faculty counterparts and urged them to meet together whenever necessary. We sidestepped the question of authority, of who was in charge of decisions on issues, and concentrated on process, on how deliberation would be conducted. That resulted in a good deal of learning, certainly by students, but also by faculty.

Controversies over social regulations were much harder to resolve. Students objected to a whole series of rules governing student conduct, from rules about where smoking was permitted, rules against consumption of alcoholic beverages in dormitories, rules about the issuance of dormitory keys to students to abolish the requirement that they return to their rooms by specified hours, and rules against having men in their rooms. Basically students rejected the principle that the faculty had responsibility *in loco parentis*. Student leaders were on the whole unwilling to compromise on these issues. Faculty wanted to maintain at least some reserve power over social rules, but students wanted all rule-making authority transferred to the Student Government Association. Attempts to design a new procedure for making and administering rules were repeatedly sidetracked by student demands for the immediate abrogation of existing rules. In the area of social rules, the division between students and faculty was tenacious and there was high impatience among students with attempts to compromise. There were no violent confrontations, but the issue continued into the next year. It was a generational conflict: students were no longer willing to accept faculty or administration control over their social lives.

CHAPTER EIGHT

I kept Meribeth fully informed about what was going on in the committees, she in turn endorsed what the committees recommended, and together we were able to persuade the faculty on nearly every issue. The background question of whether Mount Holyoke should continue as a women's college was deferred by setting up a study to survey the consequences of adopting coeducation at other colleges. Nearly every men's college became coeducational in these years, but five of the seven leading women's colleges—Mount Holyoke, Smith, Wellesley, Barnard and Bryn Mawr—continued as single-sex institutions. They found new justification for their existence for a generation of women to whom professional careers were far more open than ever before and for whom separate education built self-confidence.

In April the search for a new president succeeded splendidly with the appointment of David Truman, effective at the start of the next academic year. Meribeth Cameron returned to her position as academic dean and I was free to make plans for an upcoming sabbatical. In my report to the trustees at the end of my year as acting academic dean, I wrote that "change was orderly at Mount Holyoke during 1968–69 . . . because we were able to agree on changes in social regulations and curriculum which were satisfactory to those most concerned." But I warned that "in another year, such agreement may not be possible because of moral, academic, or financial constraints or because of divisions among students or between students and faculty more severe than any we experienced." I was quite certain that controversies on the Mount Holyoke campus and on other campuses were not over, and I hoped the trustees would continue to show the confidence in the college's faculty and administration that had been a decisive advantage during the preceding months.

> The changes made this year may have beneficial effects lasting into the near future [I wrote]. Not only have they removed some problems, but they have also helped generate a sense of community, of pride in the institution and of commitment to it. They may also have helped to preserve the sense of civility which has been conspicuous at this College in the past. These are precious assets as the College faces further demands for changes, demands that are certain to come, cer-

tain to be made with high impatience and liable to be more difficult to meet than those we encountered this year.

Although administration took most of my time and energy in 1968–69, I was simultaneously thinking about the next stage of my academic career. For many academic administrators, there is tension between the time commitments that administration requires and the abiding commitment to teaching and research that is for most faculty members the origin of their professional career. Nothing in my year in administration diminished my enthusiasm for returning to teaching and research. In my book on the German parliament I had reflected on the contrast between its failure to maintain democracy in the 1930s and its postwar success. I now wanted to expand my interest in parliaments to other countries. I wanted to focus on their role in maintaining the stability of political systems in crisis, and I had applied for a Guggenheim Foundation fellowship to supplement my sabbatical salary for the following year to make a full year's leave possible. Sixteen years out of graduate school, I also felt the need to learn new methods of political research that were spreading in the discipline. Instead of planning to spend an entire sabbatical year outside the country as I had in my previous sabbatical, I thought it would be valuable to spend at least part of it at a major research university. It was particularly attractive to consider spending it at the University of Iowa, which had a methods-oriented department and four or five faculty working on legislatures. A year and a half after the lecture I had given at Iowa in 1967, I participated in a legislative research conference there that afforded me a chance to become acquainted with a large group of scholars in this field, both from other American universities and from universities in Europe and Asia. All this sharpened my ideas about a new research project and, not incidentally, it made me increasingly aware of the attractions of the University of Iowa. I had kept in touch with John Wahlke throughout 1968. He was by then chair of the department, and he had invited me to spend my 1969–70 sabbatical year at Iowa.

I had hesitated mainly because Cornell University was developing an offer of a faculty position for me there. But just as the Cornell offer came, major student disruptions on the Cornell campus, including the armed occupation of the student union, caused uproar in the faculty and particularly in the Government Department. For half a dozen years it had been a severely fractured department, divided between a group of rigidly conservative scholars influenced by the teaching of a controversial political theorist, Leo Strauss, and those open to the many other approaches in the field. The faculty on either side of that existing division took opposite sides on the student demands on campus, which in the critical days took the form of a sharp division between those who advocated blanket amnesty for all students who had disrupted the campus and those who insisted on a judicial process. I guessed that the offer of an appointment at Cornell carried with it the hope that I would be a moderating influence in the Government Department. But I did not want to enter a badly divided department. It seemed likely that several of its senior members would leave. When the university did grant amnesty, three faculty members in the Government Department resigned immediately and its chair left several months later. Within two months the university president had also resigned. The acting department chair urged me to accept the appointment nevertheless, trying to convince me that the department would soon heal. But the appeal of returning to my Ph.D. institution, which I might have felt, was gone. Of course the department and the university did recover. However, I had always had an underlying concern, since my earliest undergraduate years, that Cornell suffered a congenital division between its privately endowed liberal arts and engineering colleges, which attracted affluent students many of whom belonged to more than fifty fraternities and sororities, and its public colleges, which offered low tuition for education in agriculture, veterinary medicine, home economics, hotel administration, and labor relations. That underlying concern contributed to my dismay at the harsh way the student confrontations were playing out at Cornell, thinking they were exacerbated by the social divisions that I had always found in the student population.

I sometimes wondered how different my life and that of my family would have been had I accepted the Cornell appointment, but I have never once regretted turning down the Cornell offer. Despite my abiding admiration for Cornell and loyalty to the university in which I had received my education, it was probably not the best place to pursue my academic career. When I received the Guggenheim Fellowship for which I had applied, I decided to take it at Iowa. Although I was not yet sure, my year as an administrator turned out to be my last year on the faculty at Mount Holyoke, though not my last year of association with that college. A year after leaving its faculty I was invited to serve on its Board of Trustees, and I was very happy in that way to maintain my bond with that institution in a new form. In the longer run, this was also not my last year in academic administration, which is the subject of chapter 11. So 1968–69 was an unsettling year, worrying as it evolved, and in the end a year of many new beginnings for me and my family.

9

Discovering Iowa

I knew very little about Iowa in the early 1960s. Even now most people outside Iowa know little about it. After living in Iowa more than half of my life, I continue to be surprised by the puzzled look I get from people when I tell them where I live. In an urban society, a state without major cities escapes attention. Before Jimmy Carter used the Iowa caucuses in 1976 to attract attention to his presidential candidacy, Iowa was even less well known than it has become. When I received a letter from the chair of the Political Science Department, in December 1964, asking whether I would be interested in a position in comparative politics, I thanked him but wrote rather evasively that "I cannot consider it at this time." And when Ina and our children and I drove through Iowa in June 1966 on our way to a summer at UCLA, we intended to stop to see Joseph Tanenhaus, a graduate school friend whom I knew to be at the University of Iowa. I drove right by Iowa City on Interstate 80 to Ames to look for him, apparently unaware that there were two universities in Iowa with two confusingly similar names: The State University of Iowa in Iowa City and Iowa State University in Ames. My friend was at the former.

Two years after I had replied to the department chair that I was not interested in applying for a position, two new senior appointments in the department made it suddenly very appealing to me. One was the appointment of John Wahlke, whose innovative role-system analysis of four state legislatures had attracted the attention of specialists on legislatures throughout the profession. His move to Iowa made that department immediately one of the centers of legislative research. I have already described that I had met him at the American Political Science convention in Chicago in the fall of 1967. He had read my book on the German parliament and invited me to give a lecture in Iowa on legislative research. The other was the appointment of Joe Tanenhaus, my friend from graduate school, whom I had missed seeing on our drive across the country. He had become a prominent member of the profession whose work I admired. On that first visit to the University of Iowa to give a lecture, he talked up the attractions of Iowa to me. The university library is extraordinary, he told me, explaining that Iowa aspires to be the third strongest university among the Big Ten and that it offers salaries commensurate with that ambition. My visit banished all kinds of preconceptions about the university and Iowa City. The younger members of the department whom I met seemed interesting and stimulating. Several of them took me to a wonderful steak dinner at a local restaurant. And I spent an evening in the beautiful living room of a contemporary architecture-designed house of a recently appointed faculty member. These were my first real impressions of what had been merely a landscape from the highway when we drove by three years earlier. Two months after my visit, Joe wrote me "to pursue in a somewhat more detailed and explicit way a subject that was cautiously broached when you were out here: the possibility of your joining this department." His letter said that "we have finally succeeded in opening a new senior line in comparative politics" and suggested that I "give serious thought over the next several days to [my] interest in coming here." He wrote that John Wahlke would become chair of the department and that he would phone me soon "to discuss these matters with you." I had several other prospects for moving from Mount Holyoke at that time, so I was not yet ready to make a decision about Iowa, but I was certainly interested.

Wahlke and I stayed in contact. When I saw him again at the American Political Science meetings in Washington, D.C., in the fall of 1968, I told him that I might be interested in spending my forthcoming Mount Holyoke sabbatical at Iowa, thinking this would be a noncommittal way of becoming acquainted with the department. He could not have been more welcoming, and wrote me a few days later "By all means, let us

CHAPTER NINE

work on the possibility of your spending some time with us next year. We should certainly bend every effort to provide you with some decent working space and conversational companions." And he added, "As I said before, and do not hesitate to repeat, we are eager to do anything we can to promote the possibilities of a more permanent connection, too." We kept up a steady correspondence. He agreed to serve as a referee for an application I had made to the Guggenheim Foundation for a fellowship to supplement the half salary from Mount Holyoke that I would receive if I took the next year as a sabbatical. Meanwhile, I had told him that I was also considering an offer of an appointment at Cornell University, which I had received after my visiting semester there the previous year. John was undeterred, persistent in keeping me interested in Iowa. When the Cornell Department fell apart in the throes of the severe campus riots there, which I have described in the previous chapter, a visiting year at Iowa with longer term prospects was more attractive than ever.

In August 1969 we rented our house in South Hadley, packed what we thought we would need for a year's visit to Iowa into the trunk and onto the roof of our Dodge Dart, and drove the 1,200 miles to Iowa City with our children aged 15 and 11 often engaging in territorial battles in the back seat. As we turned down Longview Knoll where Wahlke had found us a house to rent, I wondered somewhat anxiously what my family's reaction to Iowa would be. I had been in Iowa City twice, they never had, and we were going to be there for a year—or more. We were still in the driveway when a neighbor ran over to welcome us. The next day the wife of a colleague who lived up the street rang our doorbell to introduce herself. Right from these first encounters we saw that Iowa friendliness was not just a myth. Later it occurred to me that we were encountering something like a frontier spirit, a welcoming, mutual helpfulness perhaps inspired by living far from the urban centers of the country. We were struck by that many other times. The house Wahlke had found for us, five miles north of the city, was located on the Iowa River, with huge windows providing spectacular views of the river through the trees. It had no basement or attic, all the rooms were on one floor, and its décor was simple, modern, and very appealing. The timbered, hilly, river bank surroundings were quite unlike our preconception of the midwestern terrain. From the start every one of us was pleased, and our immediately positive first impressions were constantly reinforced in the following days and weeks.

The Department of Political Science at the University of Iowa had developed a remarkable reputation in the profession considering its small size. With eighteen faculty members, it was the smallest among the Big Ten political science departments with which it sought to compete. It compensated for its size by focusing on two fields: voting behavior and legislative studies. The commitment to focus was deliberate. While the focus on voting behavior reflected the emphasis on that field in many departments, especially among midwestern universities, the emphasis on legislatures was probably accidental, a by-product of appointments made for other reasons. Samuel ("Pat") Patterson, appointed in 1961, had done a dissertation on the Wisconsin legislature. G. R. ("Bob") Boynton, whom I mentioned earlier in the chapter on computers, had come three years later. He specialized in public opinion. Together they were collaborating on an interview study of the Iowa legislature using an innovative theoretical framework. The department had a Latin American specialist, Peter Snow, and a specialist on Korea and Japan, C. L. Kim. Both had been appointed for their area specializations although each undertook research on legislatures among other subjects. Wahlke kept publishing on legislatures after his path-breaking collaboration on *The Legislative System*. The department had only one tenured political theorist. In comparative politics it had no ambition to cover the globe but was anxious to have a senior European specialist. It was the department's strength in legislative research that made it intellectually just the right place for me. In retrospect, it was joining the Iowa Department of Political Science that enabled me to do the best work I was capable of doing.

In my first three months as a visitor, I began to understand what made the department so successful. It had made two distinguished senior appointments in the mid-1960s and they added luster to an impressive group of half a dozen younger research-active faculty who had come up through the ranks in that decade. It had adopted tough tenure standards. It was one of the three or four strongest departments in the university's College of Liberal Arts and could count on support from the administration. It had a faculty position for a visiting foreign scholar, a position that was held in my first year by a prominent Japanese political scien-

CHAPTER NINE

tist. Through a succession of prominent foreign visitors, it was known in Europe. It had an exchange agreement with the University of Istanbul that brought Turkish graduate students to Iowa and gave Iowa faculty the opportunity to spend a year in Istanbul. It had an endowment named after the department's first head, Benjamin Shambaugh, that permitted it to hold a major international research conference every three years. A conference on legislative research was the one at which I had given a paper in the spring before we came. The conference papers led to a series of books on "frontiers of research." In all these respects the department had a prominence in the profession well beyond what could be expected from its size.

It was quite self-consciously a two-tier department. One group of faculty, regarded as outstanding teachers but not particularly productive scholars, had mostly been appointed in the 1950s. A second group of more recent appointees consisted of individuals ambitious to make their mark in the national profession. These two groups respected each other. Those active in research were proud of the excellent reputation as teachers of their colleagues who had published little. Those who were primarily teachers deferred in hiring decisions to those who did outstanding research. The department was homogeneous by today's standards. It had no women members and no African Americans, although in these respects it was then typical. It had reacted against having a strong chairman after its history of having had only two "heads" for its first sixty years. It was therefore committed to having a rotating three-year chairmanship, in which every faculty member was expected to take his turn. The department was proud of its reputation in the profession and determined to maintain and improve it. In the 1969 survey conducted by the American Council of Education, the department ranked eighteenth in the nation, no mean achievement for a department of its size in a universe of nearly one-hundred Ph.D.-granting departments.

Although it had been a homogeneous, all-male department, its members were proud that its Ph.Ds. had been strikingly diverse. It had awarded its first Ph.D. to a woman in 1918 and its first to an African American in 1941. It was particularly proud of Jewel Prestage, the first African American woman to receive a Ph.D. in political science in the United States, who received her degree from the department in 1954 and then went on to be a leader in the profession. I knew Jewel from national meetings well before I thought of coming to Iowa. In the year I came to Iowa, there were a few women in the graduate program and they were among its best students.

Departmental pride gave the department an *espirit de corps*. It had the reputation, well deserved, of being the most collegial department in the country. Every faculty member in the department had an office on the third floor of Schaeffer Hall, and I was given a small office at one end. That office geography promoted constant contact among faculty. Faculty tended to work in their offices although some had library carrels to which they could escape. Few worked at home. There were regular social occasions, beginning with a daily coffee hour at 10 o'clock in which everyone not teaching at that hour participated. The discussion there turned, to my astonishment, not on politics or political science but on football, basketball, and baseball. References to current events, when they were made, chiefly cited articles in the *Des Moines Register*. From time to time the coffee hour discussion concerned departmental issues, and I began to see that decisions in the irregularly held department meetings had often been prefigured during the coffee hours. These informal social occasions reinforced an implicit hierarchy. A few leaders set the tone by force of their personalities and professional accomplishments. The department was more nearly an oligarchy than an authoritarian hierarchy, due to the rotating chairmanship.

A considerable proportion of the faculty marched down the hill together every day for lunch at the Faculty Club, a very modest facility kept alive by a few faculty members among whom the political scientists were prominent. Most Monday evenings there was volleyball, which included spouses and was followed by pizza at Shakey's, another regular occasion. The wives of faculty—none of whom were working women—included some excellent cooks. Thanks to them, there were memorable department dinner parties, at which the consumption of cocktails and wine occasionally pushed the limits. All this reinforced departmental cohesion. Everyone seemed to value togetherness, although as time went by I realized that some people found it a bit oppressive.

As newcomers Ina and I were warmly welcomed. We were treated not merely as visitors but as potential additions to the department and the community. We settled in easily, aware of our distance from the familiar east coast principally by the discovery that *The New York Times* was available only by mail, four days late. I was determined to solve that problem. In the following year I made a complicated arrangement to bring copies that the *Times* was airlifting to Chicago on to Iowa City by Greyhound bus. Several former graduate students still remember with amusement that I gave them a paid job to pick up papers at the Iowa City bus terminal and deliver them to campus for other faculty suffering from withdrawal symptoms like me. We had not lived in New York City for nineteen years but still thought of ourselves as New Yorkers. But it was "the paper" that we missed the most.

The University of Iowa was its own community, noticeably worldly in many respects. It had a resident string quartet, a new art museum, plans for a new concert hall designed by the New York firm of Harrison and Abramowitz, an impressive research library of nearly two million volumes, and notable professional schools in law and medicine. Compared to Mount Holyoke College and South Hadley, Massachusetts, the University of Iowa and Iowa City were significantly larger and attractively cosmopolitan. That colored everything new that we encountered.

I worked in my office in the department every day, became well acquainted with the faculty, had a passing acquaintance with a few graduate students, and tried not to miss the daily coffee hour. Although midmorning coffee and the white bread sandwiches at the Faculty Club were not the attraction, being so fully included in the department's social occasions meant that Ina and I found ourselves assimilated to the new environment very quickly. At my suggestion, Ina, who had just finished a master's degree in philosophy at the University of Massachusetts, introduced herself to the chair of the Department of Philosophy. Within a month he had mentioned her to the chair of philosophy at Coe College in Cedar Rapids who asked her to teach a course in each of two successive terms beginning in January.

In the days before open recruitment (let alone affirmative action), it was obvious that the department intended to offer me an appointment after a decent interval in what was formally a visiting appointment. The invitation to come as a visitor had had that clear implication. There were no formal procedures to go through. The department had appointed me as a research associate with a $2,000 stipend that supplemented my Guggenheim Fellowship and my sabbatical half-salary from Mount Holyoke. Although I was a visitor, Wahlke encouraged me to attend department meetings, perhaps to demonstrate the collegiality that marked the faculty. But one day before Christmas he told me not to attend, explaining that "Loewenberg" would be on the agenda. I knew what it meant. The day after the meeting, he called me in to talk about the terms of an appointment. Before we left to spend Christmas vacation with our families in New York, I had an offer of a tenured appointment as a professor in my pocket. By then Ina and I had no question about whether we should leave Mount Holyoke for Iowa. The challenge was only to explain it to our children, to our parents, to my Mount Holyoke colleagues, and to David Truman, Mount Holyoke's new president. Truman tried to persuade me to come back to Mount Holyoke for a year, but my mind was made up and he was very gracious and understanding. So were our parents. Our children were at first distressed not to be returning to their friends in South Hadley. It was hard to see our 15-year-old daughter Deborah, in tears when I took her ice-skating on the pond near our house thinking that would be a pleasant setting to tell her that we planned to stay. But they both had made new friends, liked Iowa City, and their initial shock did not last very long. The natural beauty of our surroundings appealed especially to our 11-year-old son Michael, who would go on spontaneous camping adventures with neighborhood friends in the rolling hills near our rented house.

Before the year was over, the student protest movement that had erupted on many campuses hit Iowa. In April students began to hold anti-Vietnam War rallies. They regarded the university as part of the establishment and made it and the bookstore in town the target of their anger over the Vietnam War. The furor that was fueled by the war was exacerbated by events on other campuses, most alarmingly by the use of National Guard troops to quell riots at Kent State University in early May, in which four students were killed. Iowa students roamed the streets at night and smashed store windows. On one occasion students occupied the administration building, on another evening an old armory annex burned to the ground, and other buildings seemed threatened. There were continual mass protest meetings. In a remarkable way

CHAPTER NINE

these events reinforced faculty cohesion. The political science, history, language, and classics faculties, which shared Schaeffer Hall, were assigned all-night fire watch on a succession of days, in the expectation that students would not attack a building in which their teachers were camping. For me that was an opportunity to meet members of the other departments in the building. In later years friends I made in the Department of History recalled the unusual circumstances of our first encounters. When several days after the Kent State shooting University President Willard Boyd gave students the option to leave the campus for the summer without waiting to take their final exams, the campus emptied quickly and the tense atmosphere evaporated. It was my first impression of the university's president, his calm wisdom, and of the state's Board of Regents, its respect for the university administration and its ability to keep its distance. It made no move to second-guess the president's handling of the student uprising. While the student protests at Cornell had severely fractured the faculty in the previous year leading me to turn down the offer of an appointment, the handling of the protests at Iowa a year later just reinforced faculty and administration cohesion, and my admiration for what was becoming our new home.

When we explored housing in Iowa City, we had become very fond of the attractive surroundings of the house we had rented for a year, our children especially so. By coincidence I had met a young architect, William Nowysz, who told me that he was eager to design residences. Ina and I did not think we could afford an architect-designed house, but we decided very cautiously to discuss the possibility with him, thinking that just conceivably he could design an affordable house to be built on a lot close to where we had rented. He did a first sketch that was such a startlingly imaginative implementation of the general preferences we had expressed in our initial discussion with him that we persuaded ourselves — to our surprise — to work with him to build a house. He agreed to a rigid budget limit. Despite warnings from friends of the risks we were taking of cost overruns and unanticipated architectural problems, it was a wonderful experience leading to a lifelong friendship with him. The house he designed gave our move to Iowa an exceptionally beautiful setting.

I was anxious to satisfy the department's expectations of me as a research scholar. More than I realized at the time, it was a substantial challenge to find myself suddenly a professor at a research university. I was eager to teach graduate students but had only limited experience with graduate education, had never had a Ph.D. student, and had only taught two graduate courses, one each as a visitor at Columbia University and at Cornell. I knew that I needed to sharpen my skills in statistics. I was at Iowa with a prestigious Guggenheim grant to work on a very general project concerning the influence of legislatures on regime stability. I had several manuscripts under way. By the example of my new colleagues, I knew I would be expected to obtain research funding and to publish regularly.

The professional challenge coincided with a number of challenges in our personal lives in our first years in Iowa. We had two teenage children, each confronting us with difficult issues. Ina was endeavoring to develop a career. Her father was seriously ill, her mother chronically so, and my mother intermittently. That we were in an unfamiliar part of the United States was not as much of a problem as people assumed. I was often asked whether it was difficult to become accustomed to the change from life in South Hadley to life in Iowa City. I found that the least of the difficulty of our move. For all their differences, they were both college towns. But the greater distance from our three surviving parents, and the stages in our teenage children's lives, together with the professional expectations the department had of me, made the transition to Iowa for all of its positive aspects more demanding than I sometimes realized. Our first years in Iowa included some unexpectedly stressful times. But as I gradually found it possible to sort out the various challenges, the enormously positive aspects of our move to Iowa, personally and professionally, for me as well as for Ina, became ever more evident.

The Iowa department was well connected in the profession. Vernon Van Dyke, its first chair after the era of department heads, had been editor of the *Midwest Journal of Political Science* and president of the Midwest Political Science Association and was at that time vice-president of the American Political Science Association; Wahlke chaired the Nominating Committee of the APSA; Patterson had just been appointed editor of the *Midwest Journal*. Joe Tanenhaus had recently coauthored a widely regarded history of the discipline. These senior scholars were leaders in American political science whose books and articles were widely known.

CHAPTER NINE

I felt the need to measure up to them. Before I knew it, a good deal depended on that, not just for me but for the department, because the two most recent senior appointees, who had been instrumental in attracting me, were gone two years after I came. Wahlke, who had recruited me, resigned as chair in a dispute with the dean before I even assumed my permanent appointment. At the end of my first full year at Iowa he had decided to leave for a prestigious appointment at the State University of New York at Stony Brook, recruited by Joe Tanenhaus who had left Iowa to be chair at Stony Brook just before I arrived. A year later a promising Soviet scholar followed both of them. Although senior salaries at Iowa were good, the demand for senior scholars particularly in newly developing departments was very great. Stony Brook was an example. What Iowa had won in the 1960s it stood to lose in the early 1970s. It was the first of many examples of the ability of the Iowa department to recruit excellent scholars but also to lose them.

However some of the most promising scholars in the department who had been appointed in the 1960s and had risen through the ranks had a devotion to it that sustained the department against prominent losses. Most important among them was Pat Patterson, who was on leave at the University of Essex in the United Kingdom in my first year but who became my closest faculty colleague in the following years. He was a mainstay of the department in every sense: a prolific author, a popular teacher of the huge introductory American Government course, and the coauthor of an acclaimed textbook on legislatures. He dropped in on his colleagues in their offices constantly, encouraging, cheering, and being attentive to problems. Bob Boynton was the department's specialist in quantitative analysis and the director of its Laboratory for Political Research. He was always ready to assist his colleagues' research. Others were doing innovative research on Latin American politics and on Japan and Korea. They all gave promise of continuing research strength in the department.

Several Iowa faculty had been active in local, state, and national politics. Russell Ross, who became chair from one day to the next when Wahlke resigned, had served for two years as executive assistant to the state governor. Another member had served a term in Congress; others were active in municipal and school politics. And many members of the department were active on university committees. The departure of the senior scholars who had first attracted me was an unexpected disappointment but it did not devastate me. It was exciting to be in the department because I had the sense of being at once in close touch with the political science profession, with state and national politics, and with the university.

The department had had a long history of training Ph.D.s from the beginning of the century and had recently reorganized its graduate program. It had placed its Ph.Ds. in a great variety of departments in the country including in some of the most outstanding. Its best graduate students added to the department's national reputation. In 1969–70 its graduate program was very large, with one-hundred students enrolled in various stages of working toward their degrees, but the department was about to cut the size of the program in half to take account of a declining number of positions available for new Ph.D.s in the 1970s. The rapid expansion of enrollment in American universities in the 1950s and 1960s was gradually coming to an end. Wahlke had designed a new introduction to the discipline of political science in the graduate curriculum emphasizing comparative politics and research methodology. I co-taught it with him in my first full year at Iowa. The new first-year program included required seminars in American politics and international relations, and a course in statistics. It became a model for other methods-oriented departments in the country. I was asked to design an introductory seminar in comparative politics and that gave me the opportunity to study the recent work on the methodology of comparative analysis. One result was a review article for what was then called the *Midwest Journal of Political Science*, which attracted a good deal of attention but, more importantly, gave me some feeling of competence in educating graduate students in the field. In the article I wrote:

> The appearance of a spate of new books dealing explicitly with the theoretical and methodological problems of comparative political research suggests that the first major reorientation in two decades is occurring in the field of comparative politics.

That sentence reflected my recognition that important developments in the field were occurring for the first time since I was in graduate school and that I needed to understand them. I inherited a graduate student whose faculty adviser had left, and he became my first Ph.D. Eventually other students earned Ph.D.s in my field, but over the years their number was small. Comparative politics never became as heavily enrolled in the department as was American politics. But for a long time I was the senior person in the field.

During the first year of my appointment, Alan Kornberg, a legislative specialist at Duke University, invited a group of Iowa faculty to a conference at a handsome research center jointly owned by Duke and the University of North Carolina at Chapel Hill. He had organized a Committee for Comparative Legislative Studies to encourage research on legislatures in developing countries. Five of us from Iowa were among twenty-seven participants. We all wrote papers that were eventually published, but a more important outcome was an application to the U.S. Agency for International Development (A.I.D.) for a grant to support further research on the role of legislatures in political development. Kornberg, who was an excellent entrepreneur, had paved the way for such a grant, and discovered that the agency needed evidence of widespread interest in such work. He therefore proposed that Duke, the University of Hawaii, and the University of Iowa, from which most of the conference participants had come, establish a Consortium for Legislative Research to sign the grant application. Back at Iowa, Wahlke was leaving; Patterson was taking on the editorship of the *Midwest Journal of Political Science*. That left me among the senior members of the department to write Iowa's share of the application. When the consortium received a $1 million grant, Iowa's share was $250,000, a substantial sum at that time. Administering it required some staff assistance and that in turn led to the need to establish a research center devoted to the project. I remember Pat Patterson saying to me, "Jerry, you have got to do that." That was all there was to it. It was the beginning of the Comparative Legislative Research Center at Iowa. Once again by accident, I fell into an administrative position, this time research administration, a responsibility meant to be consistent with full-time teaching and with my own research.

The center administered the first grant, a subsequent renewal, and subsequent grants for legislative research from the Ford Foundation, the National Science Foundation, and smaller private foundations for legislative research in other areas of the world. Since Iowa did not actually have a specialist on legislatures in developing areas, part of the grant was used to fund a faculty position for an initial two-year period, which the university subsequently made permanent. We recruited Joel Barkan, a young Africa specialist who held a recent Ph.D. from UCLA. Barkan, Kim, and Ilter Turan, a young faculty member at the University of Istanbul who had spent a year at the university in the Iowa-Turkey exchange, were the lead scholars in the center's first research project. The university's support for what we were doing reinforced my appreciation of the department's standing in the eyes of the central administration.

The initial work of the center on developing legislatures was never the focus of my own research, which continued to be on legislatures in Europe. But directing the center put me in touch with scholars doing legislative research at other universities, gave me the opportunity to invite visitors for lectures and short-term appointments, and led to some of my most important friendships in the profession—with Alan Kornberg and William Mishler at Duke, with Michael Mezey, then at the University of Hawaii, and especially with Malcolm Jewell at the University of Kentucky and Heinz Eulau of Stanford. The center became a useful umbrella for other grant applications, for administering grants, and for the issuance and distribution of what we called "Occasional Papers" reporting the results of research. They attracted some attention in the profession and gave us initial experience in research publication, which eventually paved the way for the establishment of the *Legislative Studies Quarterly*. All that was in the future but as I look back now, I reflect that the decision to accept an appointment at Iowa had so many unanticipated professional and personal consequences. My disappointment at Wahlke's departure was offset by unexpected opportunities. The impact on the lives of the four members of our family—on Ina's career, on our children's education and careers and personal lives—is a reminder that the secondary and tertiary effects of even the most careful decisions, in what was for us a remarkably stable world, are unpredictable. But we never had reason to second-guess our decision to move to Iowa.

10

Founding the *Legislative Studies Quarterly*

In the beginning starting an academic journal was a lark, a homemade enterprise growing out of the activities of the research center I was directing. It appealed to an interest in publishing that I could never shake from a very early point of my life. When I was twelve years old I bought a typewriter—my first big acquisition from my savings—and used it to type a weekly newspaper for my family, complete with an intricately typed masthead. At fourteen I composed a book on that typewriter, imitating William Shirer's *Berlin Diary*. I became the editor of my high school newspaper and was later editorial page editor on the *Cornell Daily Sun*. I headed toward the field of journalism until I was seduced by the academic life, but publishing always had a special attraction. And of course it was very relevant to an academic career, where success at a research university depended on publishing one's work. That a publication modestly begun with a small group of colleagues would become a major political science journal in partnership with one of the world's most notable academic publishers was not even remotely in my mind.

Occasionally a single conversation with a colleague can have unexpected long-term consequences. At the research conference to which the Iowa Political Science Department had invited me just before I came for a year's visit, I met Heinz Eulau, one of the most influential legislative scholars of his day. He regularly assessed the state of legislative research in the profession, published bibliographical articles, and exhorted his colleagues to undertake cumulative research. When Heinz talked about legislative research, everyone paid attention. I was with a group of conference participants and Heinz was holding forth. He was pointing out that political scientists who did research on legislatures constituted an unusually cohesive but unorganized research community whose work would be facilitated if there were a specialized academic journal in the field. Journals specialized by subfields of the discipline were still rare. That conversation did not lead to anything for the moment, but I did not forget it.

The chance to make something of it came five years later when Malcolm Jewell, who was a specialist on U.S. state legislatures at the University of Kentucky and an experienced journal editor, spent a year as a visitor at Iowa. He, too, had been at the research conference and remembered what Eulau had said. Quite casually Mac and I thought that since we were spending a year together at Iowa, the time might be right for us to try to start a specialized academic journal dedicated to legislative research. I thought we could draw on the facilities of the Comparative Legislative Research Center, which I had organized in the Department of Political Science, and on our contacts with scholars throughout the world.

We had an intellectual motive behind our interest in starting a political science journal dedicated to legislative research. We both had convictions about the direction that legislative research should go, away from its exclusive focus on the U.S. Congress that marked almost all of legislative research in the United States, and toward research comparing legislatures in various settings. That would enable research to illuminate the general characteristics of the legislative institution rather than merely its single manifestation at the national level in the United States. Mac came at that conviction from his work on U.S. state legislatures; I from my research on legislatures outside the United States, my doctoral research that involved study of the British parliament and my work on the German Bundestag. I was convinced that it is impossible to understand the legislature as a political institution without studying it in its variety across countries and levels of government. We recognized that there is great variety among the world's legislatures in how they organize themselves to reach collective decisions and how they relate to other institutions of government but that all legislatures have certain common organizational characteristics: they consist of a large number of members among whom there is no obvious hierarchy because each member is an equal representative, and they all face collective actions problems. Identifying those characteristics and solutions to those problems depends, we were convinced, on studying legislatures across many nations, many time periods, and many levels of government. We wrote in an editorial policy that we invite contributions from scholars in all countries and that our pages would be "open to all research approaches consistent with the normal canons of scholarship and to work on representative assemblies in all settings and all time periods." That turned out to be a welcome approach in a field that had been uncommonly free of methodological orthodoxies, though not of an America-centered parochialism.

We hoped to influence legislative research by devoting one issue of the new journal each year to papers given at a research conference with a common theme and by soliciting manuscripts from scholars all over the world who were doing research that could contribute to comparison among legislatures. We planned to have an international editorial board. Mac was prepared to serve as editor, and I was attracted by the entrepreneurial side of starting a journal. For me the whole project had the additional attraction of getting involved in publishing.

Although it does not occur to many faculty members in the liberal arts, there are entrepreneurial opportunities in an academic career. They consist, for example, of designing large-scale research projects and obtaining external funding for them, and of institutionalizing such projects in the form of research centers. I had done some of that after coming to Iowa and I liked doing it. Founding a research journal was an extension of that kind of activity on a slightly larger scale. I could get into publishing without the personal financial risks of being in business.

I thought that existing academic journals were hidebound in how they were published. They were conventionally typeset by old-line publishers, expensive to produce, and slow to appear. They did not employ the new methods of photo-offset printing. They were subsidized by the scholarly organizations to which they belonged so that their high cost was well hidden. Two to three years ordinarily elapsed between the submission of a manuscript and its appearance. Research papers given at conferences were typically buried in expensive conference volumes published years after the conference had taken place. I thought that if I could get some start-up funds from the University of Iowa, Mac and I could experiment with starting a more efficient legislative research journal without much overhead.

What made it enjoyable from the start and for the rest of my career was that it was a truly collegial undertaking and led to my best friendships in the profession. The Comparative Legislative Research Center I had established administered grant-supported research on legislatures in Africa, Asia, and Europe, and disseminated some of the results as "Occasional Papers," reproduced from typed pages by a photo-offset process and sent out to a list of two-hundred scholars throughout the world. Out of a combination of enthusiasm and naiveté, I thought that publishing "Occasional Papers" could quite easily be parlayed into publishing an academic journal. I imagined that the research secretary in our center could handle the whole process of soliciting subscriptions, sending out manuscripts for review, preparing camera-ready pages of the accepted manuscripts, as well as copy-editing and proofreading them. I thought the center only needed to rent some equipment for preparing the camera-ready pages and it would contract for printing copies.

Mac had been editor of the *Midwest Journal of Political Science*, forerunner of the *American Journal of Political Science*, and was therefore thoroughly experienced in editing a peer-reviewed academic journal. I had some experience in research administration, a lifelong though purely amateur interest in publishing and, ever since my childhood, an interest in budgeting. I had kept accounts of how I spent my allowance when I was in high school, and I tracked my expenditures in considerable detail when I went to college because my father gave me a check for a whole semester at a time. While living in Telluride House at Cornell, whose budget came from an endowment managed by some of the senior residents, I became acquainted with investments. For our new journal I had what later came to be called a business plan. I calculated that if we could attract five-hundred individual subscribers and five-hundred library subscriptions, subscription revenues would cover the cost of printing and

CHAPTER TEN

mailing the journal. The research secretary employed by the Comparative Legislative Research Center would serve part-time as the principal staff member for the journal. She was paid from research grants.

Mac was ready to be the editor of this new enterprise at Kentucky and I would be its publisher at Iowa. In retrospect there was an astonishing amount of bravado in my assumption that the center could handle all of the details. In fact, at the moment when we were ready to start, the center's research secretary had just resigned and we were searching for a replacement. Finding just the right person for this position now that it would entail a whole range of publishing activities was the critically important missing piece in the whole plan. Nevertheless Mac and I had decided on a speedy timetable. We planned to publish the first issue in February 1976, just three-quarters of a year after our decision to undertake it. In November 1975 we sent out an announcement of the new journal, which we named the *Legislative Studies Quarterly*, to the 13,000 members of the American Political Science Association and to 1,500 libraries. Subscription orders began to come in. We began to solicit manuscript submissions, in some cases deliberately asking prominent scholars to contribute an article for one of our early issues. For the first issue we had lined up articles by internationally known authors. We had everything except the staff to handle all the functions required since the center's secretarial position was vacant.

So for the moment we borrowed the help of faculty and staff in the Department of Political Science at Iowa and Kentucky. An Iowa student served as a part-time subscription clerk to handle the orders and to prepare a list of 1,000 potential subscribers who would get a complimentary copy of the first issue. The computer programmer in the Iowa Laboratory of Political Research wrote a program for keeping and analyzing subscriptions and printing mailing labels. Mac hired a proofreader with whom he had worked as editor of the *Midwest Journal* on his department budget. My colleague Pat Patterson, always supportive, was concerned that the new journal appear "professional," not as amateurish as the "Occasional Papers" the center had produced. "The pages have to be right-justified," he told me. I had seen a new IBM office machine that was occasionally rented in the Laboratory for Political Research to produce a data newsletter. It was an expensive electronic composer that, in addition to right-justifying text, had a memory capacity of approximately 1,000 words (or two journal pages), reflecting the modest state of composing technology in the first stages of the transition from a physical typewriter to digital composition.

I had always been interested in typography, from the time I composed homemade newsletters on my first typewriter. I thought a new journal needed a distinctive, contemporary appearance, to set it off from the conventional appearance of the established periodicals. Again borrowing available help, I asked our architect, Bill Nowysz, to design a cover for the journal and matching stationery, suggesting that the semicircular seating arrangement of legislatures was an identifiable symbol. He came up with an attractive design that we also used as our logo and never changed.

I obtained a $3,000 start-up grant from the vice president for research at the university on the grounds that we wanted to undertake a three-year research publishing experiment. With part of that grant, we rented the expensive electronic composer under an agreement that the rental cost could be applied to the purchase of the equipment. Karen Stewart, the secretary of the department, agreed to typeset the first issue in her spare time because she was intrigued by the new office machine and was always willing to pitch in on new projects. It took her three months of that spare time, which she rarely had, but at the end of that time we were able to send camera-ready pages to an out-of-state printer. In early April 1,500 copies of the first issue of *LSQ* (as we began to call it) appeared in our office, just a year after Mac and I had decided to undertake this venture.

We were still flying by the seat of our pants, entirely with borrowed help. At that moment I was rescued from the risk I had taken by my reckless assumption that the center staff could handle the publication. The center had a vacant secretarial line but the field of candidates looked quite unpromising until Karen came in one day and announced "I have another candidate for you: Mickie." Michelle L. Wiegand, the relatively new 23-year-old secretary in the department office, had been there just three-quarters of a year. I remembered she had once done a very complicated mailing for me, and I had been impressed by how anxious she was to do the job perfectly. The secretarial position in the center was one rank higher than the beginning rank she held. For that reason, and because she was also fascinated by the electronic composer, Mickie was very interested in the job. Appointing her in February 1976 turned out to be decisive for the success of the new journal. She single-handedly solved the staff problem of the *Legislative Studies Quarterly*, beginning with the second issue which appeared on time in May 1976 and ever after.

At the beginning *LSQ* seemed like a family business, with cooperation from many people in the "neighborhood." When 1,500 copies of the first printing arrived, Mickie and I stuffed the envelopes, affixed the mailing labels, and brought the heavy bundles to the post office. Karen and the department office gave some logistical support. The Laboratory for Political Research provided computer expertise and access to a card punch, a card reader, and a high-speed printer, enabling us to keep subscription records on IBM cards. Mac Jewell at Kentucky similarly had help in his department office. Mickie did everything, not only composing the final pages of each issue on the electronic composer, but keeping subscription records, corresponding with subscribers, checking the monthly university financial statements, authorizing payments, hiring a proofreader, designing advertisements, arranging exchange subscriptions with other journals, and providing a cost analysis for each issue as we carefully tracked our expenses, seeking solvency. A memorable aspect of the homemade flavor of our publication was that our tight budget did not allow us to buy all of the type fonts we needed for foreign accents and mathematical symbols. So Mickie found transparent sheets of rub-on "transfers" containing these accents and symbols at a local stationery store and rubbed them onto the camera-ready pages of the journal where they were required, one-by-one. The homemade aspect of the enterprise brought me back to the satisfaction I had from turning out a family newsletter on my first typewriter. But what quickly established *LSQ* in the profession was Mickie's aesthetic sense for the appearance of the printed page, her attention to detail, and her ability to cope with the idiosyncrasies of academic authors. As a "practical" personality, she kept my enthusiasm grounded in reality, although she turned out to be unduly skeptical about our publishing experiment when she doubted that we should be offering three-year subscriptions to our new publication.

Mac and I were determined to publish only first-rate manuscripts and estimated we could fill three issues a year on that basis. We planned to have a fourth issue annually as a conference issue on a single subject. We had the first conference issue in hand at the outset, consisting of the papers given at an International Political Science Association conference held in Malaysia in April 1975 on "The Parliamentary Politician in Asia." That conference had been sponsored by the Inter-university Consortium for Comparative Legislative Studies, which gave us a grant to publish the conference issue. We also persuaded Michael Mezey, a faculty member at the University of Hawaii, to allow us to include in *LSQ* what had been his mimeographed "Comparative Legislative Studies Newsletter." It contained regular reports on research conferences, abstracts of conference papers, and news of research in progress. Its inclusion added to the appeal of our new *Quarterly*.

The founding of *LSQ* coincided with other developments in both history and political science that confirmed the vitality of the field of legislative research. The Consortium for Comparative Legislative Research was one example. Another occurred at the 1977 meeting of the American Political Science Association, when a group of members interested in legislative studies met to organize themselves into a permanent "section" of the association. Likewise, at a meeting of the Social Science History Association, a group of members belonging to a "legislative behavior network" met to discuss their common interest in program planning and the exchange of information about research projects and findings on legislatures. These developments reinforced each other and the new journal provided an important communications link among scholars doing legislative research. The timing was right for founding a legislative studies journal. The journal greatly expanded my circle of acquaintances in the academic world.

By the end of the first year of publication, *LSQ* had ninety-one manuscripts in hand, and had a seventeen percent acceptance rate, a sign of high selectivity right from the start. Mac and I were particularly anxious to encourage comparative legislative research, to expand the field of legislative research beyond studies of the U.S. Congress. As a result of our efforts, and the direction taken by the members of our editorial board, about one-third of the manuscripts *LSQ* received in its first year dealt with state legislatures, one-fourth with the U.S. Congress, one-fourth with European legislatures, and about one-sixth with legislatures in developing countries. Therefore, a majority of the manuscripts we published in the first year were on non-American legislatures. In the political science profession, many of us associated with *LSQ* kept advocating research on legislatures outside the United States and on research comparing legislatures. Although progress away from U.S.-centered research was slow, the existence of a journal devoted to legislative and not merely congressional research contributed to that progress. After one year the journal had 500 subscribers, 300 of them individuals, 200 from libraries. Library subscriptions were growing encouragingly. The solvency of the journal depended on them since libraries were charged a higher subscription price than individuals. This was an augury of the economics of publishing academic journals a generation later, when individual scholars increasingly abandoned their own subscriptions and wanted to read journals online. As individuals no longer bought their own copies, in the digital age the solvency of academic journals began to depend almost exclusively on the sale of licenses to libraries giving their faculties online access.

I had pretended that *LSQ* was a three-year experiment when I asked for a start-up grant from the university but of course I intended it to be lasting. I had estimated that the journal could be self-supporting if it could attract 1,000 subscribers. After one year we were halfway there but only halfway, and we still needed some support. We received one more boost from the university, which agreed to purchase the electronic composer to relieve us from the rental fee, but the vice-president told us that there could be no further support from his office. He had the funds to start up promising enterprises but not to subsidize them, which imposed a good financial discipline on us. For many years the journal depended on the center's research grants. There was a mutually reinforcing relationship between publishing *LSQ* and the center's research activity, both financially and for me intellectually. My responsibility for reviewing submitted manuscripts and for writing an editor's introduction for each issue of *LSQ* helped to keep me abreast of research in the field when my own research took second place during my eight years in university administration, which is the subject of the next chapter. Eventually the journal's prominence in the profession enabled it to become entirely self-sustaining financially.

What started as a homemade enterprise with borrowed help eventually became an important academic journal that helped to shape legislative research in the United States and internationally. Thirty-five years after its founding, it had achieved the eleventh highest "impact factor" among more than ninety journals in the political science profession, a remarkable accomplishment for a journal that began so modestly. In 2010 the *Legislative Studies Quarterly* entered into an agreement with Wiley-Blackwell under which that renowned publishing firm would manage the composition, printing, and international distribution of the journal that Mac Jewell and I had started with conviction and enthusiasm but really on a shoestring. Mickie had been responsible for all aspects of the publication from the moment she started as a young secretary. Through the years as its managing editor she had been eager to keep up with the rapidly changing technology of academic publishing. Along the way she had completed her undergraduate degree in economics and obtained an M.B.A. degree. But it had become obvious in the twenty-first century that the digital production and worldwide distribution of the journal required a level of expertise that only an association with a large publisher could provide. When Mickie as managing editor and I as center director signed the agreement with Wiley-Blackwell, it marked another stage in the most successful project and the best collegial partnership of my entire academic life.

11

Unexpectedly Dean

I did not aspire to any of the administrative positions I ever held, including becoming dean of the College of Liberal Arts of the University of Iowa. The way it happened framed the whole experience for me because it never seemed like a departure from teaching and research; it seemed more like a temporary tangent. I kept finding connections between my experience as a teacher and scholar and the new challenges of "deaning." It began quite unexpectedly and turned out to be far more interesting that I could have imagined. It came at a moment when the college was ready for some important reorganization, and that gave me a chance to participate in designing new institutions of collegiate governance, which drew on my academic interest in institutional design.

It happened early in 1984. The chair of a committee searching for a new dean wrote me to ask whether I would be interested in being a candidate. I declined without hesitation. I explained that I loved teaching and that I had an agenda of research I wanted to undertake after I finished the term I was then serving as chair of my department. That would ordinarily have been the end of it. I wanted to get back to a research project on legislatures in Belgium, Italy, and Switzerland that I had not yet completed when I became the department chair two years earlier. I was enthusiastic about editing the *Legislative Studies Quarterly* that I had founded eight years before. I had postponed taking my turn as department chair as long as I could, and I was looking forward to being finished with an administrative position I had found frustrating. Our once unusually cohesive department had become seriously divided, and I found that as chair I had very little ability to influence my contentious colleagues. I really never thought of myself as an administrator, even though in one way or another I had often played that role, as department chair and acting academic dean at Mount Holyoke, as director of the Comparative Research Center at Iowa, and now again as department chair at Iowa. I was just completing thirteen years on the Mount Holyoke Board of Trustees, the last five as its chair, an unusual role for a former faculty member. But I had not sought any of those positions. I always had reservations about being diverted from my primary love of teaching and research. In early 1984 I certainly had no interest in being a candidate for dean of the college. An academic vice-president I knew had once observed that very few faculty members had what he called "an administrative temperament," and I think I was sometimes identified as someone possessing that trait. But what led me to accept these positions occasionally was my lifelong fascination for institutions of governance at all levels and a sense of institutional obligation.

That I became dean was the result of a number of coincidences. In 1982–83 I had served on a committee to prepare a self-study of the College of Liberal Arts in preparation for an external review of the college. It was my first experience at Iowa on a major college-wide committee and it was time-consuming, but I learned a lot about the college. A recurring theme in our committee report was that "the comprehensiveness of the College's educational mission is not matched by comprehensive administrative machinery." When two members of the external review committee visited the college, they recommended that it examine possible changes in its governance structure immediately, even before the review was completed, suggesting that this would be helpful in discussions with candidates for the position of dean. Because I had written the part of the self-study on the college's governance structure, I was asked to chair an "Ad-hoc Committee on the Governance of the College" and to report to the faculty on possible options within two months. Parallel to these formal preparations for making changes in the college, an informal group of faculty, calling itself the "Roundtable," was also discussing the need to reform the college's committee structure and decision-making

CHAPTER ELEVEN

procedures. The prospects for change were therefore emerging from several directions.

That the need for change was widely perceived was not surprising. During the remarkable continuity in the college's administration over the twenty-eight-year tenure of Dean Dewey Stuit, from 1949 to 1977, student enrollment in the college had tripled, increasing specialization had occurred in many disciplines, leading to their proliferation, and externally funded research had become important. But the structure and staffing of the college had changed little. Dean Laster, Stuit's successor, had also been disinclined to make changes during his six years in office. Both of them prided themselves on lean administrations. That was an article of faith at Iowa. Thus, the organization of the college was remarkably similar to what it had been thirty-five years earlier, although the college's external environment had changed greatly.

The university had a new president, James O. Freedman, who had been recruited from the College of Law at the University of Pennsylvania in 1982. In his first year he had appointed a new provost, Richard D. Remington, a biostatistician from the University of Michigan. So there had been change at the top and now there would be change in the leadership of the college. Soon after Freedman arrived on campus I had invited him to a research conference organized by the Department of Political Science because I wanted him to be aware of its high standing in the profession. Freedman and I had a good deal in common. We were both graduates of eastern private universities now living in the midwest, and we were both very interested in constitutional law and politics. Freedman had majored in government at Harvard and had a law degree from Yale. I had majored in government at Cornell and had both my undergraduate and graduate degrees from there. He was a voracious reader, had a library of more than 6,000 books, and began every conversation with me by asking "what are you reading?" He was a wonderful essayist and wrote inspiring articles on the meaning and importance of liberal education. As I became acquainted with the new president, we had occasional conversations about our shared interests, although both of us were inclined to maintain a certain formality with each other.

What happened next was perhaps not as surprising in retrospect as it seemed at the time. I got a call from the president's office on the first Friday afternoon of April 1984 asking me to stop by before I went home for the day because "Mr. Freedman wants to have a brief conversation with you before the weekend." Freedman told me that Dean Laster would resign on June 30th because of illness, which would probably be before a new dean could be appointed, and he asked me whether I would be willing to serve as acting dean of the college for two or three months until the search could be completed. He knew I was not a candidate for the position, which I presumed made it appropriate for him to ask me to serve in the interim. He wanted me to let him know by the following Monday. I talked it over with Ina that evening, and we agreed that under the circumstances I could not refuse.

While I tried quickly to learn something about Dean Laster's office, I was also aware that the Review Committee would advocate major changes in the organization of the college and its administration. There would be a new dean sometime in the next few months. The new provost, to whom the dean reported, told me in our first conversation that he was astonished how under-administered the college had been by the standards of the University of Michigan from which he had come. He said he would provide a budget for such new staff appointments as I thought necessary even before a new dean took office. I began to realize that though I would be an interim dean for only a short period, I would not merely be a placeholder preserving the status quo. What I had suddenly undertaken looked more and more like an interesting short-term assignment, involving some institution rebuilding. It could be a temporary detour that would allow me to apply some of my academic knowledge of institutions and give me a chance to help design possible changes in the college's governmental organization.

The external review committee was not shy about assessing problems or about recommending changes. Its report identified two major problems in the college: the quality of the departments was highly uneven and the administrative organization of the college made it unmanageable. One dean with a tiny staff was responsible for forty-two academic departments reflecting a particularly broad definition of what constituted the liberal arts. The dean's office had one assistant to the dean, one three-fifths time associate dean for finance, two half-time associate deans for curriculum and student advising, and four secretarial posi-

CHAPTER ELEVEN

tions. The external review committee recommended a reorganization of the college that would break it up into several "discipline based groups of departments," each with its own administrative head and budget, an increase in the administrative staff, and a reallocation of resources to strengthen those departments central to the collegiate mission.

Even before I took office as acting dean I found I needed to recommend the appointment of a new associate dean for curriculum and student advising because the two half-time associate deans were resigning. I also believed that the office needed a second associate dean to deal with faculty appointments. With the provost's approval, I chose two senior scholars for these positions, convinced that faculty respect for administrators depended on having accomplished scholars in all administrative positions.

From my previous experience as department chair I also knew that scholars — myself included — were not usually professionally accomplished administrators, and that their ability to administer any unit from the department level on up required having highly competent administrative assistants. I found no one in the dean's office who answered that description. Remington agreed to add such positions. Among the candidates who applied, I was intrigued by Mary Lou Doyle. She had held an editorial position in the School of Religion, could type 120 words a minute, and did not answer typical interviewer questions in a routine way. She told me afterwards that her friends had warned her that I was pretty conservative and that in the interview with me she should not show her offbeat side. Among the candidates she stood out as distinctive and she turned out to be a perfect match for how I saw the job. She was not only a speedy and accurate typist in days when that was a clear asset, but also an excellent organizer. She had an unflappable personality with a good sense of humor. Those were indispensable qualities as she sat outside the door to the dean's office, fielding phone calls and requests for appointments. In a position exposed to a lot of temperaments, she was amused rather than angered at the foibles she saw in people. She also had a photographic memory, was a human search engine, at least equal to the later computer versions of that ability. Mary Lou became the secret of the smooth running of the dean's office. Later we created comparable positions for the associate deans.

UNEXPECTEDLY DEAN

On July 2, 1984, I sat for the first time in the elegant office of the dean on the first floor of Schaeffer Hall, behind a large walnut desk that was bare except for an "in basket" and an "out basket." I had never before encountered that simple organization of work flow but it began to dominate my life. In most instances a person becomes dean of a large college after rising ambitiously through the administrative ranks of a university, acquiring increasingly broad administrative experience. In my case, my occasional previous administrative experience did not prepare me at all for the wide span of administrative responsibility required of the dean of Iowa's liberal arts college. The college included an exceptionally large number of academic programs: all of the sciences, the social sciences, and the humanities, as well as the performing and the graphic arts, plus a number of professional programs. At that time the dean was responsible for forty-two academic units, the college had nearly 900 voting faculty members, and it educated three-fifths of the nearly 30,000 students at the University. But as I sat there for the first time I was amazed rather than intimidated. I looked forward to an interesting, exciting experience, thinking it would be a short interval in my academic life.

I learned almost immediately that the "in basket" would fill up quickly unless I shuffled what it contained into the "out basket" throughout the day. The dean's office did not have a computer, but each of us had a terminal that had text processing capability and was linked to the university computer. I became adept at reading fast, avoiding any temptation to put something aside till later as I realized that later with spare time would never come. I learned to draft a quick response to most requests on the computer terminal for Mary Lou to transform into a proper letter. My favorite way to dispose of a request was to attach a yellow Post-it note to it indicating what I thought should be done with it and by whom. At a retirement party many years later, people in the office gave me pads of Post-its, saying they knew I would not be able to survive without them.

I took breaks to walk around among the other offices where the associate and assistant deans had desks, to become acquainted with them and with those members of the small staff who had been there with my predecessor. I needed all the help I could get. Almost from the beginning, the two new associate deans and I would start each day at 8:30 with a half-hour conversation about what was going on in general and what specific problems each of us were dealing with. We called it the caucus and it nurtured a marvelous collegiality. I came in an hour earlier while things were quiet in the office to prepare for the day. I felt pretty good about staying on top of the rapid flow of meetings and communications, but I realized also that the position would take nearly all of my time, weekend and evenings included. As long as everything was new and temporary, that was fine with me.

In the first weeks I encountered three issues that could not be simply dispatched by a memo. One department chair came to see me to complain that Dean Laster had unilaterally awarded salary increases to four faculty members, going outside the department's procedures for evaluating performance and that this had caused a furor in the department. I did not see how I could reverse what my predecessor had done, but it alerted me to the need to respect departmental procedures on the sensitive issue of assigning salaries. Another department chair came to report that two graduate students had complained about sexual harassment by a faculty member. That became an example of the responsibility the dean had for investigating, mediating, and deciding on sanctions arising from faculty misbehavior, ranging from trivial to appalling. There were established procedures for settling student misbehavior, but for violations of acceptable professional behavior by faculty, rules and procedures were rudimentary. Formal procedures for investigating complaints of sexual harassment had only begun to be developed, which meant that a dean had to intervene on an ad hoc basis. Another chair came to request the addition of a faculty position immediately, which he insisted was indispensable to meet curriculum requirements in the fall. The college's budget was supervised by a part-time associate dean who had no professional financial experience. She told me I had to make an appeal to the associate provost. The Provost's Office had kept the college on a short budgetary leash, had provided it with no professional financial officer, and had no confidence that the college could manage its large budget responsibly. That had been the practice, but the new provost wanted to get away from it. He was prepared to give the college considerable financial autonomy, but that had to wait until the college had a professional financial officer, which in turn would wait till a new dean took office.

My appointment schedule filled quickly, as did the list of telephone calls to return. Since this was before the advent of emails and instant messaging, nearly all my contacts with people could be channeled by Mary Lou. There were a number of fixed appointments—the meetings of the college's two elected committees, the monthly meeting with the forty-two department chairs, and the monthly meeting of the university's ten deans with the university president and provost. There were also fixed items on the agenda of the college: responses to the ongoing reviews of departments, three or four of which were under way when I started. One of these departments had become completely dysfunctional and required an immediate thorough investigation. The most important subject needing attention was the report of the external review of the college, to which the provost wanted the college's response. My first month as acting dean therefore gave me a broad orientation to the responsibilities of that office and to the pace of work over which one had little control. Meanwhile from time to time I would meet the candidates whom the search committee was interviewing to fill the permanent position; I answered their questions and told them that it was a very interesting job.

In early August Freedman told me that the search committee had been unable so far to agree on a candidate and that I would have to continue as acting dean for perhaps as long as the entire academic year 1984–85. He also said that he heard from all sides that I was doing a very good job, that he thought that I was enjoying it, and that I had all the qualifications for the position. He urged me strongly to consider becoming a candidate. He pointed out that it was an opportunity to exercise intellectual leadership, not just good management.

I absolutely had not anticipated that. I was still anxious to return to full-time teaching and research. But it was also true that I had found the position of dean both stimulating and intellectually interesting. If at first I thought it could be a brief busman's holiday for me, I found that I was not merely filling a gap waiting for the appointment of a new dean. I had been able to do a number of things in the office that had longer term implications. Almost daily I learned new aspects of university organization, time management, evaluating people and programs, and delegating responsibility. Most interesting was the realization that I was once again a student of the liberal arts, required to learn about many completely unfamiliar academic fields, and privileged to have department chairs as teachers who needed to be patient with me.

So after six weeks as acting dean I realized that I was intrigued by the prospect of staying on, but I was not about to decide quickly. I wanted to consult colleagues in my discipline outside the university who were or had been deans of large colleges. I talked at length with David Truman, who had been dean of the undergraduate college at Columbia University and whom I had come to know well when he was president of Mount Holyoke. At the political science meetings in early September, I talked with several faculty members in my profession who were or had been deans. They all encouraged me that being dean was an interesting job and that it would suit my abilities and my personality. I also received encouragement from many faculty members who knew me at Iowa. Ina and I talked back and forth, but she did not try to influence me one way or another. She was fully engaged in her job in financial management at University Hospitals and Clinics. I felt uncertain about whether I wanted to devote years of my life to administration. Yet it appeared that there was a connection between my academic interest in studying political institutions and my occasional forays into administering the academic versions of such institutions, however unpremeditated these forays always were. I realized that the position of dean was fundamentally different from that of a department chair. As dean one could exercise influence commensurate with the responsibility the position carried. That was not true of departmental chairs as their positions had developed in liberal arts colleges away from long-time headships. Support for change in the governance of the college was widespread and the dean would play a substantial role in channeling change. What finally persuaded me was the thought that serving as dean of a large College of Liberal Arts would be a renewal of my liberal arts education, would give me a chance to influence the organization of an institution that was ready for change, and would greatly expand my circle of acquaintants at the University of Iowa. About a month after Freedman broached the idea, I agreed to be a candidate, and about two weeks later the search committee recommended my appointment.

I had some conditions that the provost accepted in writing. I wanted to continue to do at least some teaching and to keep my hand in research and in editing the *Legislative Studies Quarterly*. In a letter to me he wrote that "I recognize your interest in maintaining your standing as a scholar and teacher in political science during the period of your deanship. As I have indicated to you, this is consistent with my attitude toward university administration, and I welcome it heartily." We agreed that for this purpose I would be allowed one day each week out of the dean's office and that I would teach one course each year. But colleagues in political science and Mickie Wiegand at the *Legislative Studies Quarterly* soon found that they could not count on me to appear a day a week in my third-floor political science office. The demands of the dean's office always had priority though I tried to hold on in political science. I did teach one large undergraduate course, sometimes with too little preparation, and I did read and comment on manuscripts for the *Quarterly*. Most importantly I wanted to limit the number of years that I would serve as dean. I was fifty-six years old and I wanted a substantial number of years back in political science before retiring. The provost said that it made no sense to accept an appointment for fewer than five years and I agreed to that. That too did not quite work out, and I ended up serving as dean for eight years. Since I was giving up a semester's research leave that had been due to me, the provost wrote that "you will receive, should you elect to return to professorial activities after five or more years as dean, a research leave . . . of one year duration." That leave turned out to be a crucially important stepping-stone back into political science.

The incremental way I became dean—first declining to be a candidate, then agreeing to fill in for a temporary period, then seeing how interesting the position was and assuming a new role in my academic life—always left me feeling surprised that I was actually doing it. Although many administrators like to complain to faculty about their jobs, I found from the beginning and on nearly every day in the following years that I did enjoy it, and I did not pretend otherwise. From my experience as dean I learned more about universities than most faculty members ever know, or care to know. It strengthened my admiration for the institution and the people in it. I regarded it then and I still regard it as a privilege to have had that opportunity, but I am also glad that it was bounded in time and did not preclude my eventual return to full-time teaching, research, and journal editing. I always looked at the experience as a tangent from my career, and I never lost the feeling that I was serving the institution just temporarily. I noticed at meetings of the deans of the Big Ten universities that my counterparts referred to their office colleagues as "my finance officer" or "my associate dean." I could never talk that way. To me it was always the College's finance officer or the College's associate deans.

The president of the Iowa Board of Regents, Marvin Pomerantz, came to see me soon after he was appointed. He was a highly successful Des Moines businessman, devoted to the University of Iowa from which he had graduated, somewhat gruff in manner, but also very respectful of faculty. I was impressed that he was interested in meeting me. What I best remember about our conversation is that he asked me how many people report to the dean of the college, a typical administrative question. When I told him that there were forty-two department chairs directly responsible to the dean, he replied, "That's impossible, you cannot do that." Although he was in no position to change that fact, he believed that at most six or seven people should be reporting to the college's principal administrator. I never forgot that conversation, because in some respects the structure that existed was impossible. Making it workable explains a good deal about both the unremitting workload of the dean and the very general level at which the dean administers the college. But it also explains the basic challenge I saw from the start in reorganizing the dean's office and the structure of college governance.

The dean's office needed to develop the capacity to set budget priorities and to set standards for faculty promotion valid across the diverse disciplines that existed in the College. To justify such a centralization of authority in a college accustomed to complete decentralization of decision making down to the departmental level, the college needed new institutions to enable the faculty to participate in collegiate governance. Unlike corporate and governmental institutions, academic institutions tend to be organized into very flat hierarchies in which the individual faculty member has a great deal of autonomy, departments have ultimate authority in their disciplines, and, especially in the liberal arts departments, chairs are at best "first among equals." I knew that from thirty years' experience as a faculty member in two very different institutions. What had made the sparse collegiate administration at Iowa work was that departments exercised extremely wide autonomy. They expected their appointment and promotion recommendations to be endorsed by the dean, they regarded their existing faculty budget lines to belong to them, and they assumed they were free to refill them whenever vacancies occurred. That was precisely what the review of the college criticized: the absence of the ability of the college to establish standards and priorities. But I realized that in two respects the dean could potentially exercise a great deal of authority: if he made some college-level decisions on budget allocations and on appointments and promotions. In developing my ideas about the reorganization of the college, I wanted to strengthen the ability of the dean to exercise that authority knowledgeably and in a manner both responsible to the faculty and perceived to be responsible. Sitting in the dean's office at a moment of opportunity to bring about change, I realized that my scholarly research on institutions was a source of ideas for designing new institutions. I realized also that I would have to be very careful to persuade the faculty to accept change. I tried to be respectful of the autonomy of departments but I encountered criticism from the start for centralizing and bureaucratizing administration. I had inherited an administrative structure that was lean beyond belief. No wonder that the relatively few administrative positions I added looked like bureaucratization!

The basic question I confronted was whether it was plausible to continue to have a single college for forty-two departments or whether it was indispensable to break it up into three discipline-based units: separate colleges for the natural sciences, the social sciences, and the humanities, as the external review committee had recommended. This was the pattern at four of the Big Ten universities at the time: Minnesota, Michigan State, Ohio State, and Purdue. The argument of the reviewers was that the college as it existed could not be effectively administered. My view, and that of all of my colleagues and of the members of the college's executive committee, was that effective administration had not been tried. We pointed out in response to the review that a division of the college would increase the expense and the problem of administration at the university level by adding three dean and their staffs. We also argued that liberal education embraced all the disciplines in the college and that dividing it would place barriers in the way of students eager to range broadly in their educations. We urged an increase in the staff of the single College of Liberal Arts to give effective administration a try. The provost agreed, so the single college remained and I had a chance to undertake a reorganization of the governance structure and what turned out to be a modest increase in the college's administrative staff.

The educational philosophy that influenced me to reject breaking one liberal arts college into three was my commitment to the liberal arts as I had learned to understand them at Mount Holyoke and as I had come to admire the expansive definition given them at the University of Iowa. I found impressive that at Iowa the liberal arts included the performing arts—music and the studio arts, cinema and writing—and professional programs closely related to the liberal arts, notably library science and social work. It was that broad definition that made Iowa hospitable, for example, to that widely celebrated program in the college, Paul Engle's Writers' Workshop. Admittedly some of the pre-professional programs in the college did not fit easily into a traditional definition of the liberal arts, or into the organization of a college of academic departments, but making it all possible was a fascinating challenge, both managerially and intellectually. It turned out to be a renewal of my lifelong interest in defining the role of the liberal arts in higher education, and it reinforced my conviction that undergraduate students were best served if they could roam across all the liberal arts disciplines without organizational barriers.

I drew on my academic interest in representative assemblies to propose a new institution to give faculty a role in governance above the departmental level. The size of the faculty had long outgrown the number of individuals who could conceivably act as a decision-making body. The college faculty met just twice a year but attendance at the meeting was usually determined by the subjects on the agenda, so that those who attended and voted were not representative of the whole college. For example, when the college's entry requirement in mathematics was up for review by the faculty of the college in the early 1980s, the decision was in effect made not by the whole 900-member faculty but by the approximately ninety faculty in the mathematical sciences, because they alone had the incentive to attend the faculty meeting when the mathematics requirement was on the agenda. That pattern was repeated many times.

I suggested the creation of a Faculty Assembly representative of the entire faculty. That was not itself controversial, but those who could not regard the college as anything other than a collection of forty-two separate departments believed the assembly should consist entirely of members elected by the departments. After extensive discussion in the college's executive committee, I proposed that each department with five or more members would select one representative for the assembly and that in addition, the faculty in each of three divisions of the faculty — the humanities, social sciences, and sciences — would elect six members to represent their collective interests. A faculty referendum accepted that proposal and as a result a sixty-member representative Faculty Assembly was created, its two kinds of constituencies emulating the bicameral structure of Congress.

There was no way to overcome the uneven quality of departments in the college, which the external review committee had rightly criticized, than by establishing an effective collegiate review of departmental tenure recommendations. For many faculty members this was a worrisome departure from the existing tradition of departmental autonomy. It required that the dean understand the standards relevant to each of the widely varying disciplines in the college and to have outside evaluations of candidates for promotion. I knew that some kind of review committee existed in most colleges and that without it the dean at Iowa had been dependent on departmental recommendations and only rarely reversed them. When I explored the possibilities with the college's executive committee and the newly appointed associate deans, we agreed that an elected promotion review committee would appear political but that an appointed committee would have to be somehow representative. After extensive discussion, I proposed the creation of an appointed six-member committee, two members from each division of the faculty, which would be purely advisory to the dean. I made the appointments to the committee after discussing them with the college's executive committee. Respect for the advice rendered by committee would have to come from the reputation of its members, and I took care to choose the most eminent faculty in the college as the first appointees. Since I thought the committee should be purely advisory, I thought that it should be a deliberative, nonvoting body. And to fix responsibility, I wanted it to be clear that the dean made decisions on promotion recommendations. From the start I found it enormously helpful to listen to the committee's evaluation of the promotion recommendations from the departments and the further discussion with the two associate deans after we had heard the committee's discussion.

As I confronted the difficulty of applying consistent standards to faculty promotion decisions in the different disciplines that existed in this large college, I thought of comparable intellectual problems I had faced in the field of comparative politics, of comparing "apples and oranges," of comparing, for example, election procedures in different countries for their degree of democracy. In the first round of promotions after I became dean, I dealt with forty recommendations. I had to learn what standards of excellence were relevant in different intellectual endeavors. I was familiar with the indicators of excellence in political science, of publications and publication venues, of the reputation of referees. But my familiarity did not extend very far. I tried whenever possible to find an analogy between the intellectual challenges I had faced as a scholar and the new challenges I faced as a dean. Achievement in the performing arts would obviously have different indicators from achievement in the social sciences. The laboratory sciences would have to be judged by different standards than the humanities. I needed knowledgeable advice, both from within the Iowa faculty and from outside, and to have procedures for getting that advice. I knew that only if standards of excellence could be applied validly across all the intellectual endeavors that existed in the college could a departmental promotion recommendation ever be rejected and explained persuasively to the department chair who had originated the recommendation. I knew that the promotion standards a new dean set would establish an important precedent that faculty were bound to watch closely. I found that when I overruled departmental recommendations in several instances, department chairs turned out by and large to be understanding if I could explain my decision knowledgeably. I usually found that a fundamental collegiality underlay most controversies between faculty and dean.

The review of the college had emphasized the need to reallocate resources to strengthen the best departments at the expense, if necessary, of departments that were either weaker or less central to the liberal arts.

But when I became dean, the college had only limited budgetary discretion because departments insisted on controlling their faculty lines and past provosts had distrusted the college's ability to manage discretionary funds. That was partly a staffing problem: the college had no budget officer other than an associate dean serving three-fifths-time who belonged to the Department of Communication Studies. Her job was merely to track expenditures on spreadsheets using a computer terminal. The most important budget decisions were authorizations for new faculty appointments on budget lines of faculty who had retired or resigned. Departments were accustomed to controlling these. My first year as dean was one of many that required budget reductions, so new lines were not available. The required reductions in the budget could only be achieved by allowing some unfilled lines to lapse. This made it extremely difficult to undertake reallocation across departments as the review of the college had urged. Since departments assumed that their faculty lines belonged to them and not to the college, refusing a department's recommendation for a new appointment on an existing line caused inevitable resentment; so did failure to fill a line temporarily when a faculty member went on paid leave.

Two factors compensated for the tight budget I faced in my first year: general faculty understanding that the tight budget was not the dean's fault, and the willingness of the new provost to give the new dean more budget autonomy than his predecessors had had. I had always found budgeting interesting. This was budgeting on a much larger scale than I had ever experienced and yet I found it a familiar challenge. As I gained experience in the budget process with the autonomy that the provost gave, I realized that I could safely overcommit the faculty budget because an authorization to a department to search for a new faculty member did not necessarily lead to a new appointment. Searches could fail, either because a department might not find a suitable candidate or because I could urge a department not to settle for a second-best candidate. After I was able to appoint a budget officer for the college the following summer, he and I regularly assigned probabilities to the chances that a particular search authorization would lead to an appointment. That enabled us to make optimum use of even a stringently limited budget. The large size of the budget made it much easier to come up with reliable probabilities than it would have been in a smaller institution. I found the challenge of tight budgets no different from generous ones.

The most contentious aspect of reallocating resources was setting salaries based on merit. This required allocating salary budgets differentially both across and within departments. Within departments the assumption was that the allocation would be made by the chair, subject only to the dean's overall review. But the dean determined the allocation across departments, based on a judgment of departmental merit. In my first year the money available for increases was just two percent of the salary budget, and yet I was anxious to assert the principle of rewarding merit. That could only be accomplished by allocating money for salary increases unevenly among departments, based on a judgment of the number of highly accomplished faculty each one had, and requiring chairs to recommend some substantial increases to their most accomplished colleagues at the cost of zero increases to others. I received vehement criticism for this policy, which exacerbated the general despair about the poor budget. But it did demonstrate my strong commitment to making qualitative judgments and that may have had a desirable effect longer term. Nevertheless some faculty reminded me forever after that they thought this had been a demoralizing misstep. I was surprised that the angriest reaction came from my own department, even though it had received a justifiably favorable allocation. I later learned that it was a general experience of deans that their own departments had the most difficult time realizing that one of their own colleagues now had responsibilities beyond the department.

From the outset I found that responsibility for the liberal arts in a large public university was an inspiring experience. My formative years as a faculty member had come in a small liberal arts college that gloried in constantly defining and redefining the meaning of liberal arts education. Iowa's president spoke and wrote elegantly about the liberal arts. What I found myself doing was coping with the challenge of organizing the liberal arts in a very large, single college, to serve not only a very large undergraduate population but graduate students in these same disciplines. The challenge was also to remember constantly that the dean could not be the boss of faculty members. The dean was better understood as their servant, facilitating their teaching and their research. The dean needed to explain respectfully and with patience when faculty expectations could not be met, drawing on the personal qualities that contribute to good teaching. What began unexpectedly became increasingly absorbing and satisfying, an expansion of my academic career for eight years, during which I won a new appreciation of the unusual characteristics of a university, the institution that makes higher education possible.

12

Not Quite Retired

Two days after I retired on June 30, 2003, the chair of my department asked whether I would teach the advanced undergraduate comparative politics course in the fall because the person to whom the course had been assigned was going on leave. He reminded me with a smile that I had offered to be helpful, if needed, after my retirement. But he was a bit apologetic, saying he guessed I had not expected him to come around so soon and that, incidentally, there was no budget line from which I could be paid. I was surprised but I actually welcomed the chance to do some more teaching and I didn't expect to be paid. The chances to teach continued. In the following years I was asked to teach with some regularity and I kept teaching about one course each term, at various levels from first-year seminars to advanced graduate courses. I did not expect a salary at all but the university insisted on paying me the equivalent of a T.A. stipend.

When you meet a fellow political scientist you have not seen for a while, the first question often is "what are you working on?" We assume in our profession that we are always — or should always be — engaged in one research project or another. But when you are about to retire, most people assume that you are tired of working. So the question often is about whether you are going to travel when you retire or move to a warmer climate or move to where your children live. I was never sure how to answer those questions because I found myself doing many of the same things after I retired that I had done all my life: some teaching, some research, more writing and publishing than I had done in many years, some editing for the *Legislative Studies Quarterly*, and some working with graduate students and with faculty colleagues. The difference was that I was free of all the constraints that organize that work before retirement: administrative duties, committee and department meetings, and fixed office hours. And so far as moving was concerned, when we decided to move some years later from the house in which we had lived for thirty-eight years, Ina and I chose to move to an apartment, not away from but closer to the university where we had spent half of our lives.

From the beginning of my work in political science, the re-creation of democracy in Germany was a recurring subject of my research. Over the years since I first undertook my study of the German parliament, I had had the good fortune to develop rewarding collegial relationships with scholars belonging to a new generation of German political scientists. That led to opportunities to give occasional seminars and lectures in Germany after I retired. The most humbling was an invitation to participate in a conference to assess the development of parliamentary research in Germany in the forty years since the publication of my book on the Bundestag, a conference that resulted in a flattering *Festschrift*. Through these encounters with students, faculty, and members of the staff of the Bundestag, I had the satisfaction of regaining an appreciation of the best qualities of the country in which I was born just before it fell into the abyss of Nazism and total war.

In the course of my career my interests in political science had become increasingly specialized. Retirement provided the opportunity to broaden my perspective again on the subject I had studied and taught, on the institutions in which I worked, and on the lives and careers of those closest to me, colleagues and members of my family. Eventually my students after retirement tended to be freshmen or senior citizens, those at the beginning of their interests and those bringing a lifetime of experience to them. I found that I could engage students in such general subjects as what it meant when the press described the American political system as dysfunctional or how an eighteenth-century constitution could be regarded as the source of all wisdom about government in the twenty-first century. It reminded me of my earliest teaching of small classes at Mount Holyoke College. When I was invited to give lectures or seminars, it was not to present new research but to offer assessments of how the field had developed. In conversations with colleagues and friends, we did not engage in shop talk about events at the moment but rather about longer term career decisions.

Yet I was still interested in new research after I retired. To accomplish it, I often collaborated with graduate students, publishing articles jointly with them. Their proficiency in the newest research methods combined well with my experience in framing research and drawing out general implications. I also still wanted to do my own writing, and in doing that I made use of the perspective I had gained from my long involvement in the study of politics. The editor of the *American Political Science Review* asked me to write an article for its centennial issue on the contribution that émigré scholars had made to the field of comparative politics, which gave me the opportunity to assess the work of European refugees in the generation before me, many of whom I had known. The editor of a series of books "On Politics," designed as "reflections on key subfields within political science," asked me to contribute a volume to that series to be called *On Legislatures*. The series editor suggested as a subtitle "The Puzzle of Representation," noting, correctly I think, that it was this enduring puzzle that explained my interest in legislatures throughout my career.

Walking between convention hotels along Michigan Avenue at an American Political Science Association meeting early in the first decade of this century, I passed Leon Epstein, a University of Wisconsin political scientist whose work I had admired ever since graduate school. He asked me whether I was finding my way around the meetings. We both shook our heads, recalling how the profession had grown in our lifetime to overflow the accommodations of even the largest hotels. But despite the expansion of the membership of the profession and of the colleges and universities in which it is practiced, and despite the proliferation of specialties and research methods the discipline uses, the basic questions that students of politics try to answer do not change. Political theorists can trace them back to philosophers in the Greek City-states. Those who focus on U.S. politics see their sources in colonial America. My colleagues in comparative politics see them in the evolution of regime types and in nation building. At a general level the subject matter of political science is unchanging. What changes is how the subject is studied. But the same nagging questions that the subject raises keep challenging us. That is why I found it possible to be fascinated by the study of politics from well before I entered college to well past the time of my not-quite-retirement.